The Land of Saddle-bags

TO DISREGARD PHYSICAL COMFORT, TO MEET EMERGENCIES, TO FACE DANGER WITH COURAGE AND COOLNESS, TO EXERCISE RESOLUTION AND INDEPENDENCE OF SPIRIT—THESE ARE ESSENTIALS TO A RIDER IN THE LAND OF SADDLE-BAGS.

The Land of Saddle-bags

A Study of the Mountain People
of Appalachia

James Watt Raine
Foreword by Dwight B. Billings

THE UNIVERSITY PRESS OF KENTUCKY

Publication of this new edition was made possible by grants from the E.O. Robinson Mountain Fund and the National Endowment for the Humanities.

Copyright © 1924 by The Council of Women for Home Missions and Missionary Education Movement of the United States and Canada

Foreword to 1997 edition copyright © 1997 by
The University Press of Kentucky

Scholarly publisher for the Commonwealth,
serving Bellarmine University, Berea College, Centre
College of Kentucky, Eastern Kentucky University,
The Filson Historical Society, Georgetown College,
Kentucky Historical Society, Kentucky State University,
Morehead State University, Murray State University,
Northern Kentucky University, Transylvania University,
University of Kentucky, University of Louisville,
and Western Kentucky University.
All rights reserved.

Editorial and Sales Offices: The University Press of Kentucky
663 South Limestone Street, Lexington, Kentucky 40508-4008
www.kentuckypress.com

Library of Congress Cataloging-in-Publication Data

Raine, James Watt, 1869–1949.
 The land of saddle-bags : a study of the mountain people of Appalachia / James Watt Raine ; foreword by Dwight B. Billings.
   p.   cm.
 Originally published: New York : Council of Women for Home Missions and Missionary Education Movement of the United States and Canada, c1924.
 Includes bibliographical references.
 ISBN 0-8131-0929-9 (paper : alk. paper)
 1. Mountain whites (Southern State)—Social life and customs.
2. Appalachian Region, Southern—Social life and customs. I. Title.
F210.R15   1997
306'.0975'091423—dc21   96-49955
ISBN-13: 978-0-8131-0929-9 (paper : alk. paper)

This book is printed on acid-free recycled paper meeting
the requirements of the American National Standard
for Permanence in Paper for Printed Library Materials.

Manufactured in the United States of America.

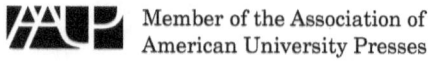 Member of the Association of
American University Presses

CONTENTS

Foreword by Dwight B. Billings ix
Preface xlv
1   Introducing Ourselves   1
2   The Spell of the Wilderness   19
3   Adventurers for Freedom   33
4   Elizabethan Virtues   65
5   Mountain Speech and Song   95
6   Moonshine and Feuds   127
7   The Mountains Go to School   163
8   The Religion of a Stalwart People   191
9   Health and Happiness   207
10   Wealth and Welfare   221
11   The Challenge   241

TO MY FATHER

ILLUSTRATIONS

In the Land of Saddle-bags FRONTISPIECE
From a Mountain Top   4
A County Seat   5
A Windowless Cabin   52
Where Rivers and Streams Abound   53
Quilts and "Kivers"   68
Cooperation and Compensation   69
When a Road Isn't a Road   148
The Secret of the Future   149
A Modern Priscilla   164
Five Miles from a Store   165
A Meeting at Wildcat Mountain   212
Reminders of Elizabethan Days   213
The Warp and Woof of Mountain Art   228
A Class in Cheese-making   229

FOREWORD

Especially since the publication in 1978 of Henry D. Shapiro's intellectual history of the idea of Appalachia, *Appalachia on Our Mind: The Southern Mountains and Mountaineers in the American Consciousness, 1870-1920,* Appalachian scholars have vigorously investigated the social origins of the notion that the mountain South is "a coherent region inhabited by an homogeneous population possessing a uniform culture."[1] With the publication of this present edition of James Watt Raine's *The Land of Saddle-bags,* the University Press of Kentucky makes available to contemporary readers one of the most important early books on mountain life, a book that has had a profound and lasting impact on how we think about Appalachia and, indeed, on the fact that we commonly believe that such a place and people can be readily identified.

The Land of Saddle-bags, first published in 1924, belongs to a genre of first-hand documentary accounts of the people and customs of the southern Appalachian Mountains that ranks second in importance only to the earlier local-color fiction of popular writers such as John Fox Jr. and Mary Noailles Murfree in constructing enduring images of the southern mountaineer that still flourish in popular thought. Among many such works published during the early decades of the twentieth century that were intended to describe authoritatively the inhabitants of the southern mountains to curious readers elsewhere, Raine's book probably ranks just below John C. Campbell's *The Southern Highlander and His Homeland* (1921) and Horace Kephart's *Our Southern Highlanders* (1913 and 1922) in importance and influence.[2]

Lacking the empirical depth of Campbell's survey of the region but less sensationalistic than Kephart's "narrative of adventure" in the Smoky Mountains of North Carolina and Tennessee, Raine's work is far and away the best "read" of these three early documentaries. Although much of his scholarship is outdated, Raine was an able literary stylist who attempted to strike a balance between broad, historical generalizations and illustrative anecdotes in his descriptions of life in Appalachia. Indeed, even the book's normally somber first publisher, the Council of Women for Home Missions and Missionary Education Movement of the United States and Canada, advertised *Saddle-bags* as a "racy book, full of the thrill of mountain adventure and the delicious humor of vigorously human people."[3]

Born to a Scottish family in London, England, in 1869, James Watt Raine, along with his father and two brothers, moved to the United States upon the death of his mother when Raine was twelve years old. Unlike many of the early interpreters of Appalachia who went there only as adults, Raine acquired early first-hand acquaintance with life in the southern mountains since his family first lived in West Virginia and later settled in Arkansas. Perhaps the experience of migrating to America from London as youths and living in the rural South encouraged the young Raine lads to be attentive to the color and character of America's diverse regions. In any event, James Watt Raine was not the only member of his family to achieve success as a local colorist. His brother William MacLeod Raine Jr. was one of the most widely read western novelists of his era, and his other brother, Edgar, a U.S. Treasury official, was hailed as "an authority on Alaska."[4]

Raine graduated from Oberlin College in 1893 and received a Bachelor of Divinity degree from Union Theological Seminary in 1897. Following brief teaching stints at Oberlin and Kansas State Agricultural College, he served as the pastor of two Congregational churches in Ohio and New York from 1897 to 1906. In 1906, he began a thirty-three year teaching career in Appalachian Kentucky at Berea College, where he first served as a professor of English literature and later as head of the English and drama departments. Raine's writings include a number of pageant plays performed at Berea College as well as a full-length biblical drama entitled *Job, the Prince of Uz,* which was also produced there.[5] In addition to the scholarly work for which he is best remembered, *The Land of Saddle-bags,* he also published a collection of mountain ballads, a modest number of academic papers, and a much less familiar short book on the people of Eastern Kentucky entitled *Saddle-bag Folk: The Way of Life in the Kentucky Mountains.*[6] Raine retired from Berea College in 1939 and died ten years later at age 79 at his hillside farm near Berea.

Significantly, the release of a new edition of Raine's book brings forth a highly influential version of Appalachia that was based upon selective images of the Kentucky mountains and on the educational agenda of Berea College. The geographer Tyrel G. Moore has shown that the early literary images of Appalachia reflected a "dominant geographical bias" that portrayed certain highly remote and undeveloped sections of the Kentucky Mountains as representative of the larger Appalachian region. Thus, for many readers outside the mountains, the highly selective descriptions of Appalachian Kentucky by fiction writers such as John Fox Jr. and social scientists such as Ellen Churchill Semple came to signify the whole southern mountain region.[7] As a consequence of this stereotyping, a "regional diversity of resources and development patterns was overlooked," according to Moore, in favor of the "perceived homogeneity of conditions in Appalachia." Raine's *The Land of Saddle-bags* certainly did not present all there was to be known about eastern Kentucky or the whole of the Appalachian region, but its Kentucky-based images of the mountain people registered a wide resonance among American readers.[8]

Besides being a prime example of the early depiction of life in the Kentucky mountains, *The Land of Saddle-bags* also admirably expresses the philosophy on Appalachia that was strongly associated with the educational mission and fortunes of Berea College, a school that came to define the mountain South as its special field of expertise and endeavor. As Shannon Wilson has shown, "Since President William Goddell Frost named the mountain region of the South 'Appalachian America,' Berea College has played a significant role in shaping the public's understanding of the region." According to Wilson, each of Berea

College's postbellum presidents (E. Henry Fairchild, William G. Frost, and William J. Hutchins), especially in their fund-raising activities on behalf of the college, represented mountain people in consistently positive terms. First, they appeared as "the heir of Revolutionary War era pioneers, defenders of the Union, [and] the rustic champions of democracy"; later as America's "contemporary ancestors," "true Americans" and "the healing solution to the divisive forces of the Civil War"; and finally, in their role as Berea students, as heroic types "overcoming appalling conditions of poverty, ignorance, and neglect to get an education and participate in the reforming of the region."[9]

James Watt Raine deployed many of these positive images and gave them his own unique discursive twists in *The Land of Saddle-bags*. A graduate of Oberlin College like each of Berea's postbellum presidents, Raine learned about Berea College and met its president, William G. Frost, while he was a student at Oberlin. After graduating in 1893, he traveled into eastern Kentucky with Frost and his wife Eleanor as they were establishing Berea's first extension program, the "Opportunity School." Soon after that, Raine became a frequent lecturer at Berea, and he probably embraced the school's philosophy of Appalachia well before becoming a member of its faculty.

To locate Raine as an academician in Kentucky, and at Berea College in particular, is to begin to situate *The Land of Saddle-bags* in the discursive space the book occupied when it was first published. Such contextualization is important since it is essential for contemporary readers to understand that *Saddle-bags* is neither a depiction of Appalachia as it exists today, nor even a "true" representation of the region at the time of the book's authorship. The point of modern scholarship on the early twentieth-century construction of Appalachia as a region in books such as *The Land of Saddle-bags* is not to deny whatever truth-value such works may contain. Indeed, an important component of contemporary Appalachian scholarship involves the re-reading and re-interrogating of classic texts on the region in order to rescue the valid first-hand observations they preserve.[10] Rather, its purpose is to show that despite their claims of having simply discovered and described the conditions of life in the southern mountains, documentary works such as this one, in fact, invented ways of seeing the southern mountains and its peoples and established traditions of writing about them as a region and cultural group with effects that are still operative today.

To point to the social origins of discursive traditions about the southern mountains and their lasting influence is to call attention to the power of writing and thus to the importance of books such as *The Land of Saddlebags* for the construction of what Henry Shapiro has called the "myth of Appalachia."[11] The mythologization of Appalachia has served many purposes. For almost twenty years now, regional scholars have called attention to how, for example, the early literary exploitation of the region paralleled and often legitimated the economic exploitation of the region's labor and natural resources during the late nineteenth- and early twentieth-century industrialization of Appalachia.[12]

Besides legitimating industrial development and the absentee control of resources, the mythologization of Appalachia has served other purposes as well, contributing often quite contradictory portrayals of the region and its people to various reading audiences over the course of its development. Thus Shapiro has examined the various organizational motivations that prompted missionaries, educators, and social workers to project positive images of Appalachia and the worthiness of its population in order to justify and secure funding for their endeavors to "uplift" there. In contrast, Shapiro notes that the writings of spokespersons for the southern textile industry depicted degradation and degeneracy in mountain farm life in order to justify child labor as a social improvement.[13] In either case, whether positive or negative images were promoted, the deployment of Appalachian discourse was an exercise of power.

Comparing the cultural construct of "Appalachianism" and Edward Said's concept of "Orientalism," Rodger Cunningham has observed that both phenomena are underlain by "a discourse of power, a way of seeing and talking about things which is conditioned by domination and which tends both to perpetuate itself and to perpetuate that domination." Such a discourse, Cunningham adds, is "a way of organizing perceptions into a closed self-referential system which takes on a life of its own, shaping assumptions and perceptions even among those who are unaware of any motivation to oppress."[14] While James Watt Raine undoubtedly viewed himself as a literary champion of the Appalachian population and certainly not as one of its oppressors, his writing nonetheless must be viewed through the lens of power relations and cultural politics.

Additional scholarship further sensitizes contemporary readers to how writings on regions worked during the era of Raine's authorship and what was at stake in them. Richard Brodhead, in particular, has enumerated the diverse functions of postbellum American regionalist literature, including local-color fiction about Appalachia. The purposes served by this immense body of literature, according to Brodhead, include not only a memorial function that took note of cultural orders passing from the current scene but also the purveyance of what he terms "stories of dominance." Such stories both described the seemingly inevitable supersession of local cultures by the new national corporate-industrial order that was then coming into being and, at the same time, implicitly asserted the social superiority of that order's new elites whose conspicuous leisure-time activities included both tourism and the consumption of local-color fiction and travelogues in orgies of reading that amounted to the equivalent of cross-cultural acquisition and imaginary annexation.[15]

James Watt Raine took exception to many of the images of mountain people found in the "picturesque stories" of local-color magazine writers, whom he described as "reasonably honest" but "temperamentally selective" and prone to "write with prolific swiftness." In an implicit critique of John Fox Jr.'s widely read short story "Hell-fer-Sartin," for instance, Raine wrote in *The Land of Saddle-bags* that he had himself "been on Hell fur Sartain" several times "during the Christmas Season" (2), only to be impressed by the "thoughtful courtesy" (3), rather than the violence, of its people.[16] But Raine, too, as Brodhead's analysis of that literary era shows, was able to take advantage of the opportunities for literary access that were provided at the time by "familiarity with cultural backwaters, acquaintance with a way of life apart from the culturally dominant," and, especially, the ability to inscribe "ethnically inflected tongues," a skill that, as we shall see below, Raine possessed to a highly refined degree.[17]

Another literary "opportunity" that proved to be of great benefit to early expositors of Appalachia, whether they were writers of fiction or of documentaries, was a national atmosphere of ethnocentrism and racism at the end of the nineteenth century. This atmosphere made tales of the "discovery" of a large, quaint, and isolated Anglo-Saxon population especially meaningful to anxious urban white readers. A number of scholars have made this point forcefully in their studies of postbellum and turn-of-the-century American literatures.

Brodhead, for one, has argued that regionalist stories of the Appalachian hillbilly, the backwoods Hoosier, the New England rustic, the Creole, and the southern black served to acknowledge the increasing cultural and ethnic pluralism of fin de siecle America by bringing readers "within hearing distance of 'the stranger within the land.'" Yet, Brodhead goes on to argue, such writing did so "first by substituting less 'different' native ethnicities for truly foreign [and therefore more threatening] ones of contemporary reality"—Appalachian hillbillies for Russian Jews, for instance—and then portraying them, especially in their use of nonstandard English, as backward and therefore tame versions of the culturally dominant groups.[18]

Other scholars have focused even more directly on the special place of Appalachian imagery in this national context of fears and anxieties. Looking at northern reappraisals of the South and southerners after the Civil War, Nina Silber has shown that "the 1890s cult of Anglo-Saxonism encouraged northerners to reevaluate all southern white people in a more approving light." In this context, the whites of the mountain South "became northern culture's cause célèbre."¹⁹ Shapiro likewise has shown how, in the 1870s, the home missionaries of northern denominations abandoned their efforts on behalf of African-Americans in the South in favor of working for the uplift of mountain whites, the latter having been falsely declared innocent of the sin of slaveholding.²⁰

Shapiro has also shown how the benefits of educational reform worked in Appalachia around 1900, especially by Berea College, were often justified to northern beneficiaries by the fact that mountain people were "a saving remnant, able by their presence 'to offset some of the undesirable foreign populations' whose presence in the United States threatened the maintenance of traditional values and patterns of culture."²¹ Many other writers as well, according to Silber, "agreed that the southern mountaineers epitomized racial purity, largely because the mountains had kept these people isolated from the waves of immigration that had polluted the racial stock of the rest of the nation."²²

Thus when contemporary readers find James Watt Raine referring to mountain people's "sterling Anglo-Saxon and Anglo-Celtic qualities" in *The Land of Saddle-bags* (260), they should not simply see Raine as reflecting the prejudices of his era but should also consider more generally how the project of constructing Appalachia was implicated in America's enduring struggle with racism and ethnocentrism. But enough about context: what exactly did Raine have to say? How do his depictions of Appalachian people, customs, and history compare to today's understandings?

To a remarkable degree, but with one prominent exception, Raine largely elaborated the story of the Mountain South as it had been narrated by William Goddell Frost twenty-five years earlier in his influential essay "Our Contemporary Ancestors in the Southern Mountains." Here, proclaiming "Appalachian America" to be one of "God's grand divisions" of the United States, Frost had called readers' attention both to the worthiness of mountain people and to the supposed geographical and cultural isolation of their region by describing the latter as "a contemporary survival" of earlier American "pioneer life." Its people, according to Frost, were only then beginning to awaken from a century-long "Rip Van Winkle sleep." As "the eighteenth-century neighbors and fellow countrymen" of twentieth century readers, these mountain people, according to Frost, still possessed the "Revolutionary patriotism" of 1776. Their "old-fashioned loyalty" to American ideals had recently been tested during the

Civil War when they "clave to the old flag" rather than the flag of the slaveholders' regime.[23] If they were benighted, it was not because they were "degraded," Frost wrote elsewhere, but because they had "not yet been graded up," a service that educational institutions like Berea College were eager to provide.[24]

Raine, himself of Scottish ethnicity, largely retold this story of a heroic but archaic people as Frost had previously described them, but he essentialized Appalachians as being predominantly Scotch-Irish in descent, thus projecting onto the ethnically and racially diverse population of the southern mountains his own identity and preference over Frost's and other writers' description of it as predominantly Anglo-Saxon.[25] These "revolutionary ancestors," Raine claimed, were primarily "descendants of the Scotch-Irish, driven from the North of Ireland by the stupidity of the Stuart kings" and subsequently "marooned on an island of mountains" in America. There they "remained very much the same" as when they fled the tyranny of British rule out of an inherent "liberty-loving spirit" (xlv, xlvi, 34).[26]

Except for his particular ethno-historical preferences, Raine's positive depiction of "the Mountain People," as he generally referred to them, was thoroughly consistent with the discursive "spin" Berean propagandists customarily gave the telling of Appalachian history in their appeals to northern benefactors.[27] This interpretation of the cultural pedigree of Appalachians stood in sharp contrast, for instance, to the widely known claims of historian John Fiske, who had contended that the "mean white class" of the South, including mountain folk, were descendants of the degraded stock of England, the paupers, criminals, and "scum of London"—an argument that, incidentally, was given renewed currency by Harry Caudill in the 1960s.[28] Raine, however, would have none of this line, expressing contempt for Fiske's assertion as simply "an erroneous statement made long ago by a careless writer" (59).

According to Raine, the "noble history" of mountain people had made lasting contributions to American life (59). Their "habit of self-reliance, of personal independence, added to their resentment at British aggression, made them inevitably resisters of tyranny" (54). These traits, he claimed, and their "leadership in the movement for American independence" (55) made mountain people major contributors to the American "idea of independence and the spirit of democracy" (53). Finally, to insure further that their worthiness was not lost to readers during what he called "these days of somewhat formidable and diverse programs of Americanization" (61), Raine concluded his paean to Appalachian virtue by claiming that "in the recesses of the Appalachian Mountains these fundamental elements of the American character are found today in stark simplicity, uncontaminated by the rush of business or the greed of money; unencrusted with social ambitions; unbroken by industrial fears. This rich deposit of true Americanism is a priceless possession, the unspoiled heritage of the American people" (62).

Raine's almost wholly positive depiction of mountain people stands in sharp contrast to the pejorative tradition of writings on Appalachia from John Fox Jr. to the present that negatively portrays Appalachian culture as a tangle of pathologies. But Raine's portrait does fall in step with the canonical treatment of Appalachian culture as being essentially static —a "retarded frontier," in the words of one of his contemporaries, or "yesterday's people," as Jack Weller described it in the 1960s.[29] Describing the habitus of mountain people as firmly fixed in the Elizabethan era, Raine wrote that "indeed, if Shakespeare could revisit the earth today, he would feel more at home among our Mountain People than anywhere else" (4). Appalachia, he proclaimed, was "the real Forest of Arden" (5).

Yet even in describing elements of Appalachian culture as archaic, i.e., as "survivals from ancestral days" (xlvi), Raine nonetheless managed to attribute a remarkably energetic and affirmative character to mountain people. They were the product of "the tremendous enthusiasm awakened by the Renaissance," whose sojourn to the New World was motivated by "magnificent imagination" along with "unconquerable energy and unclouded hope" (67-68). Consequently, Raine employed a host of descriptions throughout *The Land of Saddle-bags* to characterize mountain peoples' "Elizabethan virtues." Gifted in oratory and possessing "an unconscious dignity, a quiet courtesy" (92), mountain people were hardy, self-respecting, resourceful, independent, and honest; strongly individualistic yet hospitable and neighborly; "fresh, unjaded, [and] unspoiled" (260), and essentially "religious, if not always in practice, at least in unspoken reverence for God, the Bible, and the ordinances of religion" (75).

In only one regard did Raine detect a flaw; here, too, he followed a line set down previously by Frost in claiming that mountain people lacked "a highly developed social consciousness, a trained sense of civic solidarity"

(71). While this deficiency might easily be taken to contradict his main story line of patriotism and democratic spirit, Raine was simply lamenting the fact that because mountain people were scattered "up and down the same creek, each family like a remote constellation, revolving in its own fixed orbit," their communities possessed "no common vehicle, no fluid solvent for the easy dissemination of ideas" (173). The latter, of course, was a deficiency of social organization, not of character, which educational reform and social work were capable of remedying.

Raine's history of the mountain people was told on two levels. On the most explicit level, the sociological, Raine posited a mechanistic explanation by which the region's stasis was attributed to geographical isolation and the absence of adequate means of transportation, especially good roads. Less obvious, but probably readily apparent to Raine's readers, especially those familiar with the writings of home missionaries, was the enplotment of a moral storyline that told of mountain people's patient suffering because of this isolation and their faithful endurance of it.

It seems to have been a prominent theme in Raine's thinking—evident, for instance, in one of the few pieces of his personal correspondence to have survived—that despite the fact that innocent people often suffer great wrongs, the good in life eventually prevails though it may take looking "across the centuries" to grasp this "crumb of comfort." Raine, at least, offered this recommendation on the value of the long-run viewpoint on human affairs, and of finding in "the whole life of Jesus" a "bulwark against discouragement," as solace to an acquaintance living in England during the Nazi predations of 1938.[30] This same theme of why good and just folk may suffer yet must remain faithful was at the heart of the dramatic struggle in Raine's biblical play, "Job, Prince of Uz." Echoes of this moral position can also be found throughout *The Land of Saddle-bags*. Thus, in writing of Appalachian religion, Raine concludes that "if the faith an outsider hears voiced expresses more of resignation than of hope and joy, it is not the Mountaineer's religion that is at fault so much as the situation that bears so heavily and so unescapably upon their lives that in its clutches resignation become the primary Christian virtue" (204).

Choosing to explain Appalachian poverty and backwardness as situational rather than moral or characterological, Raine attributed the mountaineer's "accidental circumstances" (16) in large measure simply to bad roads. Believing that "civilization is primarily dependent upon good roads," not only for "channels for commerce" but for "avenues of education [and] socialization" as well (8-9), Raine contended that the "secret of the Mountain situation is that it is far off. The needs of the Mountain People are caused by their remoteness" (222). The "distance of the rural community from its agora" (66) that left mountain people "marooned" in "Elizabethan simplicity" also cut them off from the benefits of progress as well.

Because Raine described mountain culture as essentially timeless and unchanging, it is possible to read *The Land of Saddle-bags* today and not realize how rapidly and profoundly Appalachia was in fact changing during the very time Raine was writing. Although Kentucky was the last Appalachian state to be penetrated by railroads, industrialization and urbanization were rapidly transforming eastern Kentucky society in the 1920s. Coal mining in formerly remote Harlan County, for example, caused that county's population to triple between 1910 and 1920 and to double again by 1930 as laborers were drawn there literally from around the world to work in its rapidly expanding mines.[31] Minimally, at least, Raine acknowledged such changes. Noting that the "area" about which he wrote was "not constant," Raine conceded that "Whenever a river is made navigable or a railroad is built, the adjacent area gradually emerges from the Land of Saddle-bags" (xlvi).

Brodhead suggests that much local-color writing, while purporting merely to describe a regional subculture or isolated ethnic enclave, "covertly lifted it out of history, constituting it as a self-contained form belonging to the past rather than an interactive force still adapting in the present."[32] Ideologically, this literary practice had the effect of justifying the inevitable supersession of local societies and alien cultures by the newly hegemonic capitalist industrial order as well as minimizing the role of any possible local agency in either resisting change or helping to bring it about.

Raine was no apologist for the new capitalist order that was emerging in the Kentucky mountains, but his writing had the effect of making its appearance seem both inevitable and largely beyond the mountaineers' control. Although he gave little attention to that new order in his book, preferring to call attention to old Appalachia instead, Raine nevertheless deplored the fact that mountain people were "suffering from the ruthless exploitation of large financial interests." However, by writing about Appalachians as passive victims who "gazed in childlike wonder" at industrial development, he erased whatever agency they may have possessed and concluded simply that mountain people were "not at all equal to the demands of the complex civilization [then] rushing upon them." Observing that the "currents of the world's activities [were] already surging in upon them," he warned that the people of Appalachia "must learn quickly to navigate in these contending currents, or they will be swept away" (242-43).

Forced to make a "perilous leap" between the "rough, untrained farming" stage in which the settlers were mired and "the complex conditions of industrial life" that lay before them, mountain people, as Raine defined the problem, were not yet equipped to be the agents of their own regional destiny. Noting that "industrial development is always fraught with grave danger to the ideals and morals of the community," especially when "the whole community does not share" in its expansion, Raine wrote "the hazard is less when great industrial organizations grow out of the community's own internal development. But there is unspeakable danger when manufacturing, mining, and other mass operations are thrust into a backward community by outsiders. They are conducted not primarily in the community's interest, but for the benefit of the exploiters" (236). The solution to this crisis was education and community work. Mountain people, he urged, "must be hastily prepared to meet the emergency that has burst in upon them and take them by surprise. The education process must be speeded up" (244).

Appalachian scholars today reject Raine's notion that capitalism and industrialization came upon Appalachia all at once and only at the end of the nineteenth century, and they dispute the claim that mountain people had little or no influence in their course and development. By probing the early history of the region before the modern era of coalmining, timbering, and railroad building, scholars have documented indigenous roots of Appalachian capitalism and industrialism in the antebellum period.[33] The discovery of variable degrees of commercial development throughout the mountains at this early date, as well as surprisingly high levels of socioeconomic inequality there, challenges both the idea of regional homogeneity and the image of Appalachia as an undifferentiated folk society.[34] And, while scholars have indeed described ruthless exploitation and oppression in the coal mining sections of Appalachia, they have documented both labor militancy and resistance by sectors of the region's working classes as well as the existence of indigenous elites who played an important modernizing role by serving as the agents and local partners of outside capital.[35]

The recognition of economic diversity in early Appalachia has also led contemporary scholars to challenge images of the homogeneity of the region's population. The discovery that slaveholding was extensive in some sections of the southern mountains and the study of black coal miners in central Appalachia have highlighted the experience of African Americans in Appalachia, even though that group was almost completely overlooked in early accounts.[36] Half of the coal-mining workforce in the central Appalachian coalfields of southern West Virginia were European immigrants and one-fourth were African American at the very moment in time when folk song collectors were searching for traditional British ballads in the region's most remote areas. This ethnic distribution challenges the essentialistic images of mountain people as Anglo-Saxon or Anglo-Celtic folk, frozen in time, such as those who flourished in the era of *The Land of Saddlebags*.[37] Likewise, recent work on the effects of gender on the region's economic development calls attention to how Raine's neglect of gender truncates his historical vision.

Scholars remain very interested in the contributions of the Scotch-Irish population to early Appalachia,[38] and one well regarded recent work still takes that group's history as paradigmatic of the Appalachian mountain experience.[39] Today's scholars, however, no more accept James Watt Raine's story of the Scotch-Irish mountaineer as being indicative of the multicultural Appalachian experience than they accept his static image of mountain people living in Elizabethan simplicity. Making allowances for these shortcomings, however, valuable insights into turn-of-the-century life, especially in the Kentucky hills, can still be gleaned from Raine's eyewitness accounts of mountain speech and folksinging, education, religion, community, politics, and farming.

Appalachian scholars are currently debating the historical mix of commercial and subsistence-oriented farming throughout early Appalachia, but they remain divided over just how extensive and long-lasting was the pattern of self-subsistence that, until recently, was taken to be the sine quo non of Appalachian agriculture. While studies of communities in some sections of the region document the prevalence of trade and commerce, and one study virtually argues against subsistence farming altogether, others show the persistence of traditional, subsistence-first agriculture and home manufacturing in some parts of Appalachia until well into this century.[40] Raine's vivid descriptions of the everyday lifeworld of farming and home manufacturing in the subsistence-oriented farming communities of eastern Kentucky, along with the nonmarket, kinship-based forms of reciprocity that cemented them, are not generalizable to the whole region. They are probably reliable guides to many of that area's remote communities, especially since residues of this way of life have been carefully documented by other scholars at an even later date. [41]

Likewise, while failing to give attention to the full range of ethno-cultural experience in Appalachia, Raine's descriptions of the British-derived language and music of the region are also rich and evocative. As a professor of speech, drama, and English with a good ear for language, Raine had the requisite skill for local-color writing: he was able to render plausibly the quaint vocabulary and speech patterns of mountaineers to curious readers. One of the best contemporary authorities on traditional Appalachian language, Michael Montgomery, points out that Raine was "one of the best observers of mountain language in his day." His knowledge of Shakespeare, Chaucer, and Spenser, to which he frequently compared mountain speech, gave him the ability to recognize "older usages" and "provided a framework for organizing his observations."[42] While the systematic study of traditional mountain speech is still in an early phase, and linguistic scholars have warned about the shortcomings of using dialects to generalize about ethnic influences on Appalachian speech, the recent publication of new scholarly research tools is allowing progress to be made in better understanding the roots of Appalachian English.[43]

Finally and predictably, just as Raine supplied his readers with canonically expected rehearsals of Appalachian economic self-sufficiency, mountain crafts, and Appalachian song and speech, he also commented upon the region's notorious traditions of feuding and moonshine-making. Yet even describing the latter customs, which for many writers provided firm evidence of mountaineers' inherent violence, Raine downplayed both feuds and moonshine in characteristically Berean fashion.[44] While giving colorful and stereotypic accounts of both, he nonetheless stressed that "very few Mountain men make moonshine" (128). Likewise, acknowledging "a tendency to clannishness and exaggerated family loyalty" in traditional mountain society, he wisely turned his account of feuding into a discussion of the shortcomings of mountain politics (158). While contemporary scholars have not yet given moonshining the attention it possibly deserves, new scholarship on Appalachian feuding as the expression of political and economic conflicts over control of the region's resources and its direction of change make Raine's correlation of feuding with political corruption and conflict not too far off the mark.[45]

If a recent theme in Appalachian studies is "taking exception with exceptionalism," i.e., critiquing those works that have portrayed the southern mountain region as a "strange place and a peculiar people," then there is much to take exception with in Raine's *The Land of Saddle-bags*.[46] On the other hand, if the point of Appalachian studies is also to understand historically the social construction of the idea of Appalachia as well as to rescue valuable insights into the region by important writers and commentators of the past, then this classic book is well worth our continued study and appreciation.

DWIGHT B. BILLINGS

NOTES

1. Henry D. Shapiro, *Appalachia on Our Mind: The Southern Mountains and Mountaineers in the American Consciousness, 1870-1920* (Chapel Hill: Univ. of North Carolina Press,

1978), p. ix. Other book-length studies of the definition and depiction of Appalachia that contain excellent bibliographies include Allen Batteau, *The Invention of Appalachia* (Tucson: Univ. of Arizona Press, 1990); David E. Whisnant, *All That Is Native and Fine: The Politics of Culture in an American Region* (Chapel Hill: Univ. of North Carolina Press, 1983); and J.W. Williamson, *Hillbillyland: What the Movies Did to the Mountains and What the Mountains Did to the Movies* (Chapel Hill: Univ. of North Carolina Press, 1995).

2. John C. Campbell, *The Southern Highlander and His Homeland* (1921; reprint, Lexington: Univ. Press of Kentucky, 1969); Horace Kephart, *Our Southern Highlanders: A Narrative of Adventure in the Southern Appalachians and a Study of Life among the Mountaineers* (1913, 1922; reprint, Knoxville: Univ. of Tennessee Press, 1976).

3. Quoted from an undated order form/advertisement for *The Land of Saddle-bags* in Box 9-32, folder R69-II ("James Watt Raine"), Berea College Archives.

4. Biographical information on James Watt Raine and his family, though sketchy, is available primarily from press releases and obituary notices collected in a file on Raine (Box 9-32, folder R69-II) in the Berea College Archives. I am grateful to Berea College archivists Gerald Roberts and Shan-non Wilson for assistance in locating information on Raine.

5. James Watt Raine, *Job, the Prince of Uz* (Boston and Los Angeles: Walter H. Baker, 1938).

6. See his *Mountain Ballads for Social Singing: Music Collected by Cecil J. Sharp* (Berea, Ky.: Berea College Press, 1923) and *Saddle-bag Folk: The Way of Life in the Kentucky Mountains* (Evanston, Ill: Row, Peterson, 1942).

7. W.K. McNeil's *Appalachian Images in Folk and Popular Culture*, 2d ed. (Knoxville: Univ. of Tennessee Press, 1995) includes an interesting selection of early writings on Appalachian Kentucky by Fox, Semple, and others.

8. Raine did not explicitly confine his analysis to Appalachian Kentucky, noting that the mountain people's "home" was the southern half of the Appalachian Mountain chain

below the Potomac and Monongahela rivers, but virtually all the specific place names he mentions were located there. Remarks in Raine's funeral service by the Reverend Elmer Gabbard suggest that he was very familiar with the Kentucky hill country but it is not possible to determine where his observations took place or just how extensive they were.

    9. Shannon H. Wilson, "Window on the Mountains: Berea's Appalachia, 1870-1930," *The Filson Club History Quarterly* 64, no. 3 (July 1990): 384, 400.

    10. See Kathleen M. Blee and Dwight B. Billings, "Reconstructing Daily Life in the Past: An Hermeneutical Approach to Ethnographic Data," *Sociological Quarterly* 27, no. 4 (1986): 443-62.

    11. Shapiro, *Appalachia*, 263.

    12. Don Askins, "John Fox, Jr.: A Re-Appraisal; or With Friends Like That, Who Needs Enemies?" in *Colonialism in Modern America: The Appalachian Case*, ed. Helen Lewis, Linda Johnson, and Don Askins (Boone, N.C: Appalachian Consortium Press, 1978); Rodger Cunningham, "Signs of Civilization: *The Trail of the Lonesome Pine* as Colonial Narrative," *Journal of the Appalachian Studies Association* 2 (1990): 21-46; and Darlene Wilson, "The Felicitous Convergence of Mythmaking and Capital Accumulation: John Fox, Jr. and the Formation of An(Other) Almost-White American Underclass," *Journal of Appalachian Studies* 1, no. 1 (Fall 1995): 5-44.

    13. Shapiro, *Appalachia*, especially 157-85.

    14. Rodger Cunningham, "Appalachianism and Orientalism: Reflections on Reading Edward Said," *Journal of the Appalachian Studies Association* 1 (1989): 126.

    15. Richard H. Brodhead, *Cultures of Letters: Scenes of Reading and Writing in Nineteenth-Century America* (Chicago: Univ. of Chicago Press, 1993), especially chapter four, "The Reading of Regions." I am grateful to Richard Angelo for pointing out the value of Brodhead's work for this introduction.

    16. Compare to John Fox Jr., *Hell-fer-Sartin and Other Stories* (New York: Harper and Brothers, 1897).

17. Brodhead, *Cultures of Letters*, 116, 136.
18. Ibid., 137.
19. Nina Silber, *The Romance of Reunion: Northerners and the South, 1865-1900* (Chapel Hill: Univ. of North Carolina Press, 1993), 143.
20. See Shapiro, *Appalachia*, especially chapter two; also Silber, *Romance*, 143-58. On the false characterization of Appalachia as outside the zone of slaveholding and other assumptions about the prevalence or absence of racism there, see John C. Inscoe, "Race and Racism in Nineteenth-Century Southern Appalachia: Myths, Realities, and Ambiguities," in *Appalachia in the Making: The Mountain South in the Nineteenth Century*, ed. Mary Beth Pudup, Dwight B. Billings, and Altina Waller (Chapel Hill: Univ. of North Carolina Press, 1995), 103-31. For arguments against the myth of solid unionism in Appalachia during the Civil War and an analysis of how economic interdependencies shaped sectional allegiances there, see Kenneth W. Noe, *Southwest Virginia's Railroad: Modernization and the Sectional Crisis* (Urbana: Univ. of Illinois Press, 1994).
21. Shapiro, *Appalachia*, 120.
22. Silber, *Romance*, 144.
23. First published in the *Atlantic Monthly* in 1899, Frost's essay is available to contemporary readers in McNeil, ed., *Appalachian Images*, 91-106. Quotations are from 93, 92, 98, and 99.
24. William G. Frost, "The American Mountaineers," address at the Old South Church, Boston, January 14, 1900, published in *Berea Quarterly* 4, no. 4 (February 1900): 12.
25. See especially Ellen Churchill Semple, "The Anglo-Saxons of the Kentucky Mountains: A Study in Anthropo-geography" (1901), republished in 145-74 in McNeil, ed., *Appalachian Images*.
26. In one very telling passage, however, despite otherwise narrating the history of mountain people as the history of the Scotch-Irish in the mountains, Raine writes: "It is, of course, not quite accurate to speak of the characteristics com-

mon to them as racial, since the Mountain People are not all from one race or nationality. Broadly speaking, however, they constitute a race, built up of like-minded folk from the among the English, French, Germans, and Scotch-Irish" (67).

27. Even Raine's title was borrowed from an article by Frost entitled "In the Land of Saddle-bags," *Missionary Review of the World* 24 (January 1901), as cited in Shapiro, *Appalachia*, 322.

28. Quoted in Shapiro, 95; also see Harry Caudill, *Night Comes to the Cumberlands: A Biography of a Depressed Area* (Boston: Little, Brown, 1962).

29. Compare George Vincent, "A Retarded Frontier," *American Journal of Sociology* 4 (1898): 1-20, and Jack E. Weller, *Yesterday's People* (Lexington: Univ. Press of Kentucky, 1965).

30. See Raine's letter to "Mrs. Watson" in Dorset, England, dated October 12, 1938, in Berea College Archives file.

31. See John W. Hevener, *Which Side Are You On? The Harlan County Coal Miners, 1931-1939* (Urbana: Univ. of Illinois Press, 1978).

32. Brodhead, *Cultures of Letters*, 121.

33. See Wilma A. Dunaway, *The First American Frontier: Transition to Capitalism in Southern Appalachia, 1700-1860* (Chapel Hill: Univ. of North Carolina Press, 1996), and articles in Robert D. Mitchell, ed., *Appalachian Frontiers: Settlement, Society, and Development in the Preindustrial Era* (Lexington: Univ. Press of Kentucky, 1991) and in Pudup et al., *Appalachia in the Making*.

34. On inequality and its impact on development, see Mary Beth Pudup, "Social Class and Economic Development in Southeast Kentucky, 1820-1880," in Mitchell, ed., *Appalachian Frontiers*, 234-60; also, Robert Tracy McKenzie, *One South or Many? Plantation Belt and Upcountry in Civil War-Era Tennessee* (New York: Cambridge Univ. Press, 1994). For reinterpretations of "traditional" Appalachian culture that recognize accommodation and resistance to development, see Helen Lewis, Sue Kobak, and Linda Johnson, "Family, Reli-

gion, and Colonialism in Central Appalachia: Or, Bury My Rifle at Big Stone Gap," in Lewis et al., *Colonialism in Modern America*, 131-56, and Blee and Billings, "Reconstructing Daily Life." For the importance of gender in Appalachian culture and development, see Mary K. Anglin, "Lives on the Margin: Rediscovering the Women of Antebellum Western North Carolina," in Pudup et al, *Appalachia in the Making*, 185-209.

35. Compare Ronald Eller, *Miners, Millhands, and Mountaineers: Industrialization of the Appalachian South, 1880-1930* (Knoxville: Univ. of Tennessee Press, 1982), and John Gaventa, *Power and Powerlessness: Quiescence and Rebellion in an Appalachian Valley* (Urbana: Univ. of Illinois Press, 1980), with David Corbin, *Life, Work, and Rebellion in the Coal Fields: The Southern West Virginia Miners, 1880-1922* (Urbana: Univ. of Illinois Press, 1981), and Hevener, *Which Side Are You On?* Also see Eugene Conti, "The Cultural Role of Local Elites in the Kentucky Mountains: A Retrospective Analysis," *Appalachian Journal* 7 (Fall/Winter 1979-80): 51-68.

36. The pioneering work on slaveholding in Appalachia is John C. Inscoe, *Mountain Masters: Slavery and the Sectional Crisis in Western North Carolina* (Knoxville: Univ. of Tennessee Press, 1989). On African Americans in the Appalachian coal fields, see Ronald Lewis, *Black Coal Miners in America* (Lexington: Univ. Press of Kentucky, 1987), and William Trotter Jr., *Coal, Class, and Color: Blacks in Southern West Virginia, 1915-1932* (Urbana: Univ. of Illinois Press, 1990). For general information, see William H. Turner and Edward J. Cabbell, eds., *Blacks in Appalachia* (Lexington: Univ. Press of Kentucky, 1985). For an analysis of racial differences in rural nineteenth century Appalachia, see Kathleen M. Blee and Dwight B. Billings, "Race Differences in the Origin and Consequences of Chronic Poverty in Rural Appalachia," forthcoming in *Social Science History*.

37. On the ethnic composition of southern West Virginia coal mining communities around World War I, see Mack H.

Gillenwater, "Mining Settlements in Southern West Virginia," in *West Virginia and Appalachia: Selected Readings,* ed. Howard Adkins, Steve Ewing, and Chester E. Zimolzak (Dubuque, Iowa: Kendall-Hunt, 1977), 132-58. For an important discussion of the cultural politics that surrounded preferred versions of Appalachia, including its music, see Whisnant, *All That Is Native.*

38. See, for example, chapters in Tyler Blethen and Curtis Wood, eds., *Ulster and North America: Trans-Atlantic Perspectives* (Univ. of Alabama Press, forthcoming).

39. Rodger Cunningham, *Apples on the Flood: The Southern Mountain Experience* (Knoxville: Univ. of Tennessee Press, 1987). Additionally, David Hackett Fischer also traces what he interprets as essential Appalachian cultural practices to Scotch-Irish and other north English border people in *Albion's Seed: Four British Folkways in America* (New York: Oxford Univ. Press, 1989) but he has been vigorously criticized by Appalachian scholars in a special issue of the *Appalachian Journal* entitled "Culture Wars: David Hackett Fischer's *Albion's Seed,"* vol. 19, no. 2 (Winter 1992).

40. Altina Waller, in *Feud: Hatfields, McCoys, and Social Change in Appalachia, 1860-1900* (Chapel Hill: Univ. of North Carolina Press, 1988), argues for the prevalence of subsistence agriculture in the Tug River borderland of West Virginia and Kentucky until the beginning of the twentieth century, but Durwood Dunn, in *Cades Cove: The Life and Death of a Southern Appalachian Community* (Knoxville: Univ. of Tennessee Press, 1988), documents the importance of commercial agriculture much earlier in that community. See Dunaway, *First Frontier,* for a strong but controversial assertion that subsistence agriculture was almost nonexistent in the region.

41. James Brown documented the remnants of the subsistence farming way of life in the 1940s in the "Beech Creek" communities of eastern Kentucky in *Beech Creek: The Social Organization of an Isolated Kentucky Mountain Neighbor-*

hood (1950; reprint, Berea, Ky.: Berea College Press, 1988); Dwight B. Billings and Kathleen M. Blee described how that system flourished and declined in the same communities during the nineteenth and early twentieth centuries in "Agriculture and Poverty in the Kentucky Mountains: Beech Creek, 1850-1910," in Pudup, et al., *Appalachia in the Making,* 233-69.

42. Michael Montgomery, correspondence with author, 4 April 1996.

43. On the problem of using dialect differences for generalization, see Michael Ellis, "On the Use of Dialect as Evidence: *Albion's Seed* in Appalachia," *Appalachian Journal* 19, no. 3 (Spring 1992): 278-97; on the relative contributions of British and Irish varieties of English to Appalachian grammatical patterns, see Michael Montgomery, "The Roots of Appalachian English: Scotch-Irish or British Southern?" in *Journal of the Appalachian Studies Association* 3 (1991): 177-91, and "The Scotch-Irish Element in Appalachian English: How Broad? How Deep?" in Blethen and Wood, eds., *Ulster and North America.*

44. Dwight B. Billings and Kathleen M. Blee, "Where the Sun Set Crimson and the Moon Rose Red": Writing Appalachia and the Kentucky Mountain Feuds," forthcoming in *Southern Cultures.*

45. See Waller, *Feuds,* for a brilliant social history of feuding in relation to the politics and control of economic development.

46. Dwight B. Billings, Mary Beth Pudup, and Altina Waller, "Taking Exception with Exceptionalism: The Emergence and Transformation of Historical Studies of Appalachia," in Pudup et al., *Appalachia in the Making,* 1-24; see Will Wallace Harney's 1873 *Lippincott's Magazine* article, "A Strange Land and a Peculiar People," in McNeil, *Appalachian Images,* 45-58.

PREFACE

The Mountain People are the inhabitants of the region whimsically, but happily, called Appalachia. They are the descendants of the Scotch-Irish, driven from the North of Ireland by the stupidity of the Stuart kings. By the time the Declaration of Independence was signed they constituted one sixth of the population of the American colonies. They arrived in such shoals that they could not be assimilated by the sparse population of the colonies. Being of pioneer mettle, they naturally surged beyond the western limit of settlements and civilization. There were fierce Indians to the west and fiercer French, so they turned southward and swarmed down the inviting Valley of Virginia, in the heart of the mountain region. In this migration they swept along with them Palatine Germans, Protestants driven out after the Thirty Years' War, Huguenots similarly driven out of France, the more adventurous Quakers from the western reaches of Pennsylvania, and a good sprinkling of Virginia English. These latter were the less conservative element—the restless young blood, bolder unconventional spirits, men rebelling against the routine of commerce, some of plebian and some of gentle blood. They preferred the free life of the wilderness, hunting, trapping, and exploring. From these pioneers the Mountain People sprang.

While the rest of the nation has grown far from our revolutionary ancestors, the Mountain People have been marooned on an island of mountains, and have remained very much the same as they were at that time.

Does the area that I have called the Land of Saddle-Bags cover all this Appalachian region? Formerly it did, but not today.

All sociological progress is the result primarily of passable roads. The interchange of products and of ideas, and even the infusion of new blood, are all contingent upon transportation. Wherever the currents of contemporary life can flow in, or seep through, all the different human elements blend into a composite, in which the characteristics are shared in common. Whenever a river is made navigable or a railway is built, the adjacent area gradually emerges from the Land of Saddle-bags.

All these survivals from ancestral days are like prized heirlooms, with their own quaint atmosphere of dignity and romance. But they are rapidly disappearing. Yet under all changes the fundamental qualities persist. In the colossal task of Americanizing America we can wish for nothing better than these simple virtues of the pioneer, who has always been hardy, honest, hospitable, and fearless.

JAMES WATT RAINE

BEREA, KENTUCKY
January, 1924

Introducing Ourselves

Introducing Ourselves

THE backwoodsmen were Americans by birth and parentage, and of mixed race; but the dominant strain in their blood was that of the Presbyterian Irish—the Scotch-Irish as they were often called. Full credit has been awarded the Roundhead and the Cavalier for their leadership in our history; nor have we been altogether blind to the deeds of the Hollander and the Huguenot; but it is doubtful if we have wholly realized the importance of the part played by that stern and virile people . . . the pioneers of our people in their march westward.

THEODORE ROOSEVELT
The Winning of the West

CHAPTER ONE

Introducing Ourselves

ONE infers from the picturesque stories in the magazines that the Southern Highlander or Appalachian Mountaineer is in person tall, hairy, gaunt, and loose, his joints apparently tied together with bits of string. His garments consist usually of trousers and the remains of a shirt, surmounted by an enormous flapping hat. As to occupation, he is represented for the most part as sitting rather permanently on a rail fence gazing at very intelligent and well-dressed visitors; or, more sketchily, running a moonshine still; or shooting down his enemies in a feud. For which purposes he is picturesquely decorated with an old muzzle-loading squirrel rifle nearly six feet long, and the powder horn and deerskin pouch used by his grandfather.

Of course I am not personally acquainted with all the Mountain People; but for thirty years the circle of my acquaintance has been steadily enlarging, and this composite picture from the magazines does not fit very many of them. I would not say that magazine writers have a malicious intent to deceive. They are doubtless reasonably honest, but they are also temperamentally selective, and write with prolific swiftness. Men that habitually carry their pencils at half-cock, and are so eagerly sensitive to fresh impressions, are naturally startled when they see the unusual conditions in which some of us live, and hear the peculiar names our places bear. Who could write a commonplace paragraph about a news item from Beefhide, Mad Dog, Barefoot, Jamboree, Hogskin Creek, Burning Springs (a well of natural gas, discovered in early days), Contrary, Poor Fork, Viper, Traveler's Rest, Hell fur Sartain, Troublesome, Kingdom Come, Disputanta, Fish Trap, Squabble Creek, Quicksand, Cutskin, Feisty or Hazard? These naturally overstimulate the fertile imaginations of literary men, and the colors of their sketches are instinctively heightened; or perhaps, by mere natural selection, what is gray and dull and average fades out and the residue of color "strikes fiery off indeed."

Perhaps you have read a popular author's brilliant little thumb-nail etching called "Hell for Sartain." I have been on Hell fur Sartain several times myself during Christmas season. Once I was riding alone on the east side of the river, which was frozen solid on each bank, but the strong current kept it clear of ice in the middle of the stream. Meeting a man whose square saddle-bags suggested that he was a physician, I said:

"I suppose I'm on the right road for Hyden?"

"Yes," he replied, and then, stopping his horse, he called after me: "Are you acquainted with the fords in the river?"

"Why, I—I've been over the road once."

"Well, I reckon maybe you'd as well cross the river back here, and shun the quicksand up yonder."

Would a stranger find more thoughtful courtesy in the streets of Chicago or Washington?

Of course there are plenty of killings in the mountains. The doctor was then on his way home from attending a young fellow who had been "stobbed" by another. Such casualties are a natural consequence of "celebrating" Christmas. This term has a meaning not found in Webster, a deliberate intention to drink one's self into hilarious and glorious exultation.

And the day before I had met a dead man on the headwaters of Squabble Creek. Some eight or ten grim-faced men were walking or riding beside a "slide" where on an armful of cornshucks lay the body, a gray blanket spread over it. They were taking it back home to his father and mother, fifteen miles away. More celebrating! It was startling to meet death in this raw and un-hearsed fashion. Yet I met a great many men that were not dead.

On another occasion, it was growing dark, I was riding a strange mule, and forded the swollen river with some difficulty. Turning up on the farther shore of the river, I started across Hell fur Sartain Creek. I was unable in the dusk to see where the road emerged from the creek on the opposite side. The mule sank to his belly in the quicksand, while I slipped off his back, and, having larger feet, waded safely to the bank. After I had rescued the mule, I found the path, followed it through a cornfield and reached a house. Making a place for me at the roaring fire, the master urged me to stay all night, while his wife arose quickly to cook me some supper. But it was necessary to reach the county seat that night, so as soon as the moon was up I rose to leave. The host called to his fifteen-year-old son to saddle the gray mule and guide me back across the dangerous creek and the swollen river, and get me safely across Baker's ford, two miles farther up the river: "A man cain't handily cross thar, less'n he knows whar the bottom is." The lad conducted me across the three fords and bade me good night, adding in response to my hearty thanks—for it would have been an insult to offer him money—"Well, ye better go home with me and stay all night."

Perhaps you would call that boy ignorant. It is true he never saw a railway, or an electric light, or a kitchen sink, or water piped into a house. But neither did Shakespeare ever see any of these things. Indeed, if Shakespeare could revisit the earth today, he would feel more at home among our Mountain People than anywhere else. His mother cooked on an open fireplace like ours. She used the same spinning wheel; wove her home-

FROM A MOUNTAIN TOP

One beholds the majesty of the hills covered to their very summits with a dense growth of pine and walnut, oak and hickory and bass. Here, among the mountain mists, men have laboriously cleared the forests by hand and planted cornfields, often on places too high and steep to plow with horses.

A COUNTY-SEAT FORTY MILES FROM THE RAILROAD

There is a court-house, a church, a store, a telephone line, and a "hoe-tel," but there are no sidewalks, roads, lights, or water. The place is never really congested except on court-days or days of "protracted meeting," when people crowd in from the country.

spun on the same rough-hewn loom; lighted her house with the same grease-lamp, and sang her children to sleep with the same old ballads that our Mountain women use today.

Have you ever thought, when rummaging in an attic, how delightful it would be, by some Aladdin's magic, to visit the home that your great-great-grandfather built after he left this Elizabethan England and came to America? In imagination you can explore the solid old house with its home-built furniture and enjoy the quaint charm of pioneer life, long, long past.

But in our Mountains it is not past. Here we are still among Shakespeare's people. This is the real Forest of Arden. From the old log house where I live upon the outskirts of this forest, we can ride in four hours into the seventeenth century.

After a few miles on the smooth dirt road, the hills begin to squeeze closer together, their slopes grow steeper, and we turn up Napier's fork, a narrow glen with a stream at the bottom. The sides, now rocky, now park-like, are covered with luxuriant foliage to the very top. Our "road" runs along the side of the creek, crossing and recrossing it continually, and sometimes, where there is no level space on either side, the road runs for several hundred yards in the bed of the stream itself, thus "fording it eendwise." In one day's journey you may ford the river a hundred times;

or you may "take up" a "branch" or "fork" or "trace" to its source in a spring near the top of a ridge, then follow the trail across the ridge, through the "gap," till on the other side you come upon another little brooklet, which you follow down till it empties into a larger stream. Then you go up or down its bank till you come to "the third left hand holler," and so on—up and across and down—all day. No wonder "salt gits mighty expensive time hit's hauled sixty miles." And when, on a steep hillside, the path is blocked by a fallen tree or a landslide of earth and rocks, we must let our horses pick their way through the underbrush down to the creek and wade down its bed.

The creek is very steep, it is full of rocks or boulders two to three feet high, it is swollen with melted snow. Such traveling is certainly interesting, but neither safe nor comfortable, and progress is very slow. The horse gropes for every foothold, and you wonder each time whether he has found bottom or whether he is stepping on a submerged boulder, and will slip two feet deeper and perhaps throw you over his head. Going down stream, his head is considerably lower than his tail, even when he does not slip or stumble. After you have succeeded in thus running the rapids of the St. Lawrence on horseback, you feel rather proud of your horsemanship. It is quite different from your well-groomed ride in the park at home. Naturally, when you stop for dinner at the mouth of the branch, with ill-concealed elation you tell your hostess of this daring ride. But she quietly remarks, "Yes, the road's a plum sight. I went up thar to the store yesterday—hit's five mile back, I reckon you come apast hit. Well, I was clean out o' bakin' powders, and Susie broke my needle—I'm sewin' her a frock, and I jest had to git another—so John slapped the saddle on the mare, and I tuk a basket of eggs to do my tradin' with, and them eggs got powerful heavy afore I got thar because my baby was restless."

"Your baby! You don't mean that you carried a baby and a basket of eggs up and down that stream on a side saddle?"

"Shore," she smiles. "Well, no, I never brung the eggs back, I traded them," she corrected, with the usual regard for the exact truth.

And this ride, which you will remember your life long as a daring adventure, is her usual method of getting her groceries!

But another surprise awaits us. It rains all night, and next morning all the snow is melted from the hillsides. "Is that roar the noise of water?" "Yes, sir, they's a big tide in old Greasy; come out and see. Hit's over the step-rock." And sure enough, everything is under water to the very door. The volume of water in the creek is ten times what it was when we went to bed. The water swirls past fiercely, sweeping along on its muddy surface logs, tree-tops, somebody's boat, a cow still alive and pitifully moaning. Our horses could never swim that water, and our clothes would be soaked if they could. No traveling today!

Now we begin to realize how important roads are to human progress. They are not only channels for commerce, but the avenues of education, socialization, and civilization. In such weather, of course, the children cannot go to school, and in this rough country (the adjective refers to geographical conditions) there are often more absent marks than any other on the school record. Interrupted attendance is fearfully discouraging to both teacher and pupil, and it is not strange that many pupils drop out altogether when they can barely read and write. Only those endowed by a propitious fate with the ability to "take larnin' easy" can successfully make such roads a highway to learning.

Now, we understand why funerals occur in the late summer or fall. Of course, burial takes place immediately, but there can be no "funeral" until the weather is good, and roads "air fitten to travel." Then the kinsfolk and friends can gather and the favorite preacher "kin labor successf'ly to honor the appintment."

It is such conditions of belated travel that sometimes cause ludicrous complications. Our friend Felix lost his wife one winter, and the following fall, when Marthy's funeral would naturally have been preached, her brother was away in Ohio. The next year Felix himself was involved at the adjoining county seat in a long-drawn-out trial. So when the funeral did finally occur, Felix was sitting in the chief mourner's place with a new wife by his side, and as the preacher rose to the heights of pathetic eloquence, Felix sobbed upon the shoulder of his new wife for the death of Marthy. In such geographic conditions Puck, who is not dependent upon good roads, can play his mischievous pranks, which make such fools of poor mortals.

With all due respect to modern education, and to the invention of printing behind it, with all due respect to modern inventions, and to the steam engine back of them, *civilization is primarily dependent upon good roads.* Martin Conway remarks that civilizations have always arisen upon the meeting places of ideas. And ideas do not meet unless the men who think them can get together.

The isolation is even worse for the women than for the men. Men take out logs, go to the monthly Court at the county seat, drive cattle, and occasionally go to earn some "cash money" at "public works" (by which is meant any enterprise employing a number of men, such as building a courthouse or a bit of railway, work at a sawmill or at a coal mine). When there is a house-raising in the neighborhood, the women congregate and have a quilting. But such gatherings are not very frequent, and the steep hill slopes rising on all sides shut women in to a lonesome life. "I'd love to git to a place once whar I could see a big passel o' land that hadn't been stood up on edge like," said one woman out of her experience of precipitous and imprisoning horizons. Where hills are somewhat rounded, a "house-seat" is often chosen upon one of the knobs. But in the sharper and steeper valleys the only place level enough to build on is at the edge of the creek, and as there is a little larger level where a branch runs into the creek, there we usually find the home, with a "picketin'" fence around all the level land. This rich silted soil forms the garden.

The house is probably built of logs, perhaps two cribs, one roof extending over both, making a covered passageway between, with an outside chimney at each end. One crib of logs was built first, perhaps without a window, and as the family grew the house was enlarged and "improved" by building the second crib. A porch overgrown with vines or roses runs all along the front, a smoke-house stands near by in the rear, the cave-like hole beyond the smoke-house is the family coal mine. The barn is across the branch, a log crib in the center with shed roofs on all sides. At the edge of the branch just outside the picket fence is the big iron wash kettle and the "battling" bench for the family laundry. Upon it lies the batler or batlet such as Shakespeare's Touchstone sentimentally kissed. There are apple trees near the house, and perhaps a few peach trees, and along one side of the garden paling stand fifteen or twenty bee-gums.[1]

The "woman"—that is, the wife—tends the garden after it has been plowed and fitted. She raises onions, potatoes, sweet potatoes, corn, beans, tomatoes, and sometimes squash. She raises a few chickens and geese and fattens a few hogs. She dries apples and corn and shucky beans. The latter she strings with a needle and thread, and hangs overhead. She cans tomatoes and blackberries, raises a patch of sorghum and makes molasses. She barters eggs and honey and feathers at the store for sugar, salt, coffee, needles, thread, and various feminine trinkets. Some women in the remotest coves have never had a dollar in their own hands. Many of them have never been more than a few miles away from the place where they were "borned."

Some of the children make their way out to the settlements to work or to school. But those who have no ambition for an education or professional training are likely to marry young and settle down in the woods higher up the creek, where "his"

[1] So called because each hive is made from a thirty-inch log sawed from a hollow gum tree. These are set on end upon a smooth rock or slab, and are covered with split shingles or a thin flat stone.

father gives him land if he will clear it. The wife is perhaps sixteen or fifteen or, in an extreme case, thirteen. Such a couple has very little money or property to start with. But her mother says, "They're pretty well fixed. He's got some potatoes and corn and some hay and a nag. And he's got a bed (bedstead) and she's got a bed (feather bed). And he's been off workin' at public works and got a leetle money for gittin' some tricks and fixin's for the house. For pore folks that's a right smart to start on."

Of course, many mountain homes have "brought-on" furniture. Organs are not uncommon, and even formidable kitchen ranges are brought in by some adventurous agent and sold at an exorbitant price. One is frequently confronted by framed family portraits, as lifeless and ugly as any in Indiana or Pennsylvania.

But whether the people are "jest pore folks" or "right prosperous," whether they live on a passable road or in the remotest valleys, "in the head of the holler," there is often an air of plenty and comfort. Their patriarchal simplicity does not mean penury.

Their free and lavish hospitality is not strained or forced. It is the natural expression of open minds and generous hearts. It does not depend upon how much they have to offer. They are a hardy and self-respecting race. None of the men considers it a hardship to lie down and sleep wherever night may find him, in a feather bed or in the woods. They eat whatever food comes to them with the same superiority of mind. I have never seen a Mountain man that was a glutton, but have often been impressed by their abstemious habits. This superiority to mere comfort, this cleanness from the temptings of luxury is an inherent characteristic of the Mountain People. I have never known Mountain folk to refuse to extend hospitality from any false shame at the bareness of the fare or the meagerness of the accommodation. "We're pore folks, we hain't got much, but you're welcome to what there is." "If you can stand our fare, jest he'p yerself." And after this no more apologies. They have an inherent self-respect which instinctively and unconsciously feels that what is good enough for them is good enough for an accidental guest.

I once stayed overnight in a home where the mother was in bed in the front room with a week-old baby. In the lean-to kitchen at the rear the half-grown daughters cooked supper. The table was small and would not hold everything they prepared for us—fried chicken, fried ham, fried eggs, potatoes, beans, corn, tomatoes, coffee, sweet milk, buttermilk, cornbread, hot biscuit, butter, apple preserves, honey and layer apple pie.[1] Then the eldest girl, constantly swinging a "fly-bresh,"— a branch from a lilac bush,—kept passing the vari-

[1] The progenitor of the strawberry shortcake.

ous dishes and urging us to "try to mek out a meal." After the men and half-grown boys had eaten, the women and children had their supper, while we sat on the porch and talked under the starry sky. After the dishes were washed, the girls and children, bringing the small glass lamp without any chimney, climbed up the ladder into the loft to sleep. I and the old man who was guiding me were assigned to the unoccupied bed in the front room, while the host lay down with the mother and baby. But the baby was restless, and the host walked the floor with it and at intervals fed it paregoric. Perhaps this situation strikes you as funny. It seemed to them quite natural. In the Mountains hospitality is a sacred and glad duty, no matter in what predicament the family may be. This man was patriarchal in his simple, pioneer living—patriarchal also in his whole-hearted hospitality.

Nor is this hospitality merely occasional, when a chance traveler comes along. Stopping at another home, I saw the old grandmother cowering over the fire in a shawl, as she sat in a low hickory splint chair, smoking her pipe. "How are you, Mrs. Browning?" "I ain't no 'count much. But I hain't no right to complain. I've had my health for nigh onto sixty years, but now I'm foolish[1] and kind o' drinlin'. But all I want in this world's a chance to git to a better."

[1] Frail.

When Mrs. Browning was a young woman, with only five or six children, word came that a neighbor woman up the next creek was very sick. Mrs. Browning went to her at once. "Miz Browning, I'm a dying woman, and I bin wantin' mightily to see ye. I bin a-watchin' ye and I've noted that your perfession and your practice hits,[1] so I'm goin' to give ye my six children." As soon as the mother died, Mrs. Browning brought the children home. It was not even necessary to consult her husband. Eighteen months later another woman died and left her six more orphans, as another tribute to her real Christian character. Her husband's only remark was, "Where ye goin' to put 'em all, Bettie?" "Oh, there's allus room for a few more, and the big 'uns can help wait on the least ones." She reared them all with her own children, and I do not suppose she ever saw a hundred dollars. Now she is modestly hoping for a chance to get to a better world!

It is time to pause a moment to remark that there are just as many different kinds of people in the Mountains as there are outside, whether you consider them morally, mentally, socially, or financially; or consider their skill, energy, disposition, or culture. It is practically impossible to make any interesting statement that would be true of

---

[1] A term from weaving. Coverlids are woven in strips thirty-six inches wide, and two strips are sewed together. Sometimes the pattern does not "hit."

three million people. What applies to people far up the creeks and coves does not apply to those on the rich farms along the river bottoms. What is true of folk marooned on inaccessible mountain tops is not true of folk living in towns with all the resources of communication and transportation. But, wherever they go and whatever they do, the fundamental traits of the Mountain People crop out, as do those of Scots, or Jews, or any other race.

The only help I can give toward understanding and appreciating these people is to point out the traits that are fundamentally and vitally characteristic. I ask you to note those Anglo-Saxon and Anglo-Celtic qualities which you must not ignore nor obscure, if you would rightly appreciate the Elizabethan simplicity, the power and the manhood of the Mountain People. Accidental circumstances usually catch the attention of the casual observer. But circumstances are not of dominating importance. The important question here, as with any people, is, how does the man act in these circumstances? Does he master them? or do they swamp him? And when he moves into other circumstances, does he quickly adjust himself and master them too? Such examples of these Mountain People as Daniel Boone, John Sevier, Patrick Henry, Chief-Justice Marshall, and Abraham Lincoln forbid a supercilious judgment.

The Spell of the Wilderness

The Spell of the Wilderness

WITHIN the boundaries of this territory are included the four western counties of Maryland; the Blue Ridge, Valley, and Alleghany Ridge counties of Virginia; all of West Virginia; eastern Tennessee; eastern Kentucky; western North Carolina; the four northwestern counties of South Carolina; northern Georgia; and northeastern Alabama. Our mountain region, of approximately 112,000 square miles, embraces an area nearly as large as the combined areas of New York and New England, and almost equal to that of England, Scotland, Ireland, and Wales.

JOHN C. CAMPBELL
*The Southern Highlander
and His Homeland*

CHAPTER TWO

The Spell of the Wilderness

THE Appalachian Mountain chain extends along the Atlantic coast from the Gulf of St. Lawrence to the low lying lands on the Gulf of Mexico. It is cut almost in half by the two rivers—Potomac and Monongahela. The southern half of this mountainous country is the home of those people variously referred to as "Southern Highlanders," "Southern Mountaineers," or "Appalachian Mountaineers." They usually call themselves "Mountain People."

Some thirty years ago this sweep of territory crossing so many state lines was whimsically but happily named "the State of Appalachia." It is about six hundred and fifty miles long and two hundred miles wide, being half as large as Germany or France. Along its eastern edge stretches in a northeasterly direction the Blue Ridge Mountains, while the Cumberlands and Alleghenies stretch along its western edge. Between these two ranges lies what was often referred to in earlier days as the Valley of Virginia, but this central depression, a Paradise of beauty down which the increasing stream of explorers and settlers flowed, is really a series of elevated valleys, the most famous of which are the Shenandoah and the Holston. There are more mountains in Appalachia, the valleys are deeper and more frequent, the surface rougher and the trails steeper than in any other section of our country. A journey of fifty miles almost anywhere in Appalachia has far more ups and downs, and steeper ups and deeper downs, than a five-hundred-mile journey across the Rocky Mountains. One writer has described it as follows:

"The Blue Ridge is not especially difficult: only eight transverse ridges to climb up and down in fourteen miles, and none of them more than two thousand feet high from bottom to top. Then, thirteen miles across the lower end of the valley a curious formation begins.

"As a foretaste, in the three and a half miles crossing Little House and Big House Mountains, one ascends twenty-two hundred feet, descends fourteen hundred, climbs again sixteen hundred, and goes down two thousand feet on the far side.

"Beyond lie steep and narrow ridges athwart the way, paralleling each other like waves at sea. Ten distinct mountain chains are scaled and descended in the next forty miles. There are few "leads" rising gradually to their crests. Each and every one of these ridges is a Chinese wall magnified to altitudes of from a thousand to two thousand feet and covered with thicket. The hollows between them are merely deep troughs."[1]

From the Atlantic as far west as Montana, Wyo-

[1] Kephart, *Our Southern Highlanders*, p. 20.

ming, and Colorado there is, outside of Appalachia only one peak six thousand feet high. It is Mt. Washington in New Hampshire. And you can count on your fingers all those that are over five thousand feet. But in Appalachia there are more than forty peaks over six thousand feet, besides forty miles of unnamed "saddles" or dividing ridges that attain that altitude. In North Carolina alone there are twenty-one peaks higher than Mt. Washington; and in the whole of Appalachia there are nearly three hundred peaks over five thousand feet high, besides three hundred miles of saddles and ridges. These mountains of Appalachia are crowded so close together that there is comparatively little level land.

While this rough, broken steepness is, perhaps, the most noticeable physical feature of the country, the second characteristic is unquestionably its wonderful growth of forests. Here is the finest and largest body of hardwood timber in the United States. The mountains are green to their very summits, with a thick growth of trees and underbrush. There are few bare rocks or naked cliffs. And even the peculiar "bald" that is occasionally seen on the crown of a mountain is green with an excellent natural grass. There are usually many shades of green in the great variety of trees; and color is a winsome and peculiar quality of the landscape. In the spring the delicate tan fluff of the beeches, the red flowering of maples, the feathery white blossoms of the "sarviss," are succeeded by the redbud's blaze of purple that covers the whole hillside, which after a week's triumph is kindled into renewed freshness by the jets of white dogwood that flicker through it.

Higher up the mountain the delicate orange of the azalea startles us like tongues of flame, and a little later the waxy pink of the laurel, and the superb glory of the rhododendron stretches away for hundreds of enchanted acres. These have scarcely vanished before the coves are golden with the blossomy yellow of the chestnut, and we are lifted into Elysium by the fascinating fragrance of wild grape blossoms. As we climb one of these mountains from valley to summit on a summer day, we can find successively all the wild flowers of the eastern United States in a profusion unknown elsewhere. In the fall of the year the autumn foliage lights up these mountains with a many-hued magnificence of color that no other region can rival—while above, in the magic blueness of a mysterious sky, the ever-burgeoning clouds reflect all the silken tintings of the celestial hosts.

These marvelous forests are as valuable as they are beautiful. They are the virgin forests of the new world and contain the finest hardwood timber of America. Black walnuts are so plentiful, and so easy for the carpenter to work, that they have been used very freely, not only for gunstocks and furniture, but for common uses. In taking down an old barn, built of thirty-foot logs, I found walnut logs among them; when I tore up the porch floor of my old log house, I found that the planks were black walnut; and in repairing old fences, we occasionally find a walnut rail.

White and yellow poplars grow sometimes six to nine feet in diameter, and their trunks are sixty or seventy feet to the first limb. Chestnuts are even thicker, although not so tall. White oaks grow to enormous size. Groups of hickory, maple, chestnut oak, lynn, beech, birch, and hemlock fill the forests. Scattered in infinite variety are sycamore, elm, gum, buckeye, basswood, cucumber, sourwood, locust, ash, holly, cedar, persimmon, and pine.

A lumber company buys seventy thousand acres of forest. It keeps its own railway busy hauling out the lumber it cuts. "It will take twenty-five years to cull out all the large timber, and by that time there will be another growth ready to cut." Perhaps there will, but in most places it looks doubtful as one sees the wasteful methods of lumbering, the frequent forest fires, the utter carelessness of the future, the universal callousness to the country's needs in timber, water supply, and reforestation.

Appalachia, with these wonderful forests, is also remarkably well watered. Innumerable springs, swelling into ever-present branches, creeks, and forks—navigable for the most part only on horseback—empty into rather shallow rivers. But when these are swollen by "tides," they carry countless rafts and millions of logs to the sawmills. As I traveled up one creek, a man told me he had "splashed out" thirteen thousand logs that season.

A creek is usually too shallow to float logs down to the river where they can be assembled into rafts. At some suitable place, between high banks, a splash dam is built. Square cribs of logs are filled with great stones, and a dam is built against these anchored piers. In the middle is set an enormous gate or door. One side of this pushes against two projecting logs in the gateway of the dam. The other side is held in place by the trigger, a long slender log like a telegraph pole, arranged on somewhat the same principle as the figure "4" trap-triggers that boys set to catch rabbits. This dam makes a long and deep lake, into which the logs are thrown.

This done, they wait for a "tide." The most sudden tides are the result of heavy rains back in the mountains, when there are a few inches of snow. Then, overnight, creeks will swell to ten times their volume of water and rush down, a strong sullen stream. This is the long expected moment. The logs that are in the creek-bed or on its banks will be quickly carried away.

When all is ready, the trigger pole will be

thrown up, the gate released, and the dammed-up water, with its freight of logs, will rush through the dam with the roar of an avalanche, sweeping the logs down to the river. Men work with intense energy to roll into the stream those logs that lie farther back, so that the oncoming waters may carry a continuous current of logs. The feverish haste keeps up until the waters of the creek subside, as rapidly as they rose, and the tide is past.

In sharp contrast to the frequency of streams is the scarcity of lakes. There are no large lakes in the whole region, and very few small ones. Much more characteristic of its geography than the pellucid deeps of mountain lakes are its cascades, rapids, and waterfalls. For the most part, the streams are swift with rapid and sudden fall. A fall of five hundred feet in forty miles is common, even in streams of considerable size. In small streams, a fall of five hundred feet in a mile is not rare.

In spite of the great rainfall, the absence of lakes and ponds and the quick drainage furnished by these swift streams, together with the constant breezes, reduce the humidity. The climate is mild and bracing. While the sun's rays are hot, one is always comfortable in the shade, and a blanket is needed at night.

This network of little streams running down every valley determines the avenues of travel, for the roads or paths follow the watercourses. You "take up" a stream for a mile or two, now on one bank, now on the other, sometimes in the bed of the stream itself, until you come upon its source, a spring near the top of the mountain. You go on to the top, and on the other side, a few hundred yards down, you come upon another spring, which you follow till it empties into another creek or branch. This necessary custom of making the paths along the streams accounts for the peculiar directions the inquiring traveler receives: "Ye take up the left fork for half a mile, and then hit's the second right-hand holler; ye foller the branch till ye come whar ye can mighty nigh see a haystack on a sort o' clift above the road. Wa'al, jest afore ye kin see that haystack, ye cross the branch and go through a patch o' saxifras and take up Peter's Trace till hit turkey-tails out into a lot o' leetle forks that head up in coves agin the saddle. Wa'al, right thar ye cross the gap, and ye're on the headwaters of Leetle Laurel. Ye'll find hit's jest six miles." I have forded the Middle Fork of the Kentucky River a hundred times in a journey of sixteen miles.

The rapid fall of the streams offers unlimited water power which is used on the small creeks to turn tub-mills or overshot wheels. On the larger streams it is sometimes dammed up and used for factories.

Although there is no coal in the Blue Ridge or Eastern Belt, there is more coal in Appalachia than in the seven chief coal-producing countries of Europe. As one follows the paths along the creeks, coal crops out, often in very thick seams. The workable coal area is estimated (by the United States Geological Survey) to be about one eighth of the total coal area of the United States. It is at present supplying nearly one fourth of all the bituminous coal.

Iron is found in such quantities that Appalachia ranks second in importance among the iron districts in the amount of ore produced. The juxtaposition of coal and iron ore in this region, thus cutting the time and cost of transportation and handling, constitutes a great additional advantage.

Marble, mica, and asbestos, building stone, kaolin, and fire clay, copper, gold, and corundum are profitable mineral resources.

The Mountain region is suited in soil and climate for the production of nearly all the grains and fruits of the temperate zone. It grows to perfection wheat, barley, oats, corn, sorghum, timothy, clover, peas, beans, potatoes, asparagus, sweet potatoes, tomatoes, cabbage, celery, apples, pears, peaches, plums, cherries, blueberries, blackberries, and strawberries. But the lack of transportation is disheartening and discourages improvement and production. The market for such stuff is "a million miles away." The only products worth raising (aside from one's own living) are those that can walk to market—cattle, sheep, horses, and turkeys. Large droves of turkeys are driven in the autumn fifty or a hundred miles to market.

Agriculture is often very primitive. What could you expect with fields tilted at an angle of forty-five degrees? And the farmers in the past have had little assistance. The Agricultural Colleges of the various states have comparatively few Mountain students, and naturally their instruction is, for the most part, adapted to the problems presented by the characteristics of the farm lands of their own state. Most of the agriculturists have never even been in the Mountains and would not know what to do with a farm steep enough to be the hypotenuse of a triangle. It is entirely possible for a man to fall out of his cornfield and break his neck. I have a field up under the cliff that has been in corn for seventy-five years, yet is too steep to plow. It is planted and cultivated with the hoe. Parts of it are so steep that the only safe plan is to hoe the row from the bench up to the cliff, then slither down and climb up the next row. Sometimes an enterprising man buys a bale of heavy wire, fastens one end to a tree on top of the mountain, stretches it down, and fastens the other end below. He puts pulleys on the wire, from which at "gathering time" he hangs sacks of slip-shucked corn and lets them slide down by gravitation. When I asked an old man why he preferred "cushaws" (a large crook-neck squash) to pumpkins, he spat reflectively and answered, "If we growed punkins up in yan cove, they'd break loose and roll down and kill somebody. So we plant cushaws so they kin hook theirselves onto the cornstalks and stay thar." In spite of his turn for humor, he did not exaggerate the situation.

One rainy spell I noticed a great raw area where a large landslide had evidently just occurred, and as I mentioned it at the house where I stopped for dinner, a man recalled with a chuckle a similar "slip." "You remember Pete Bolin? Pete were a quar-turned, droll-natured feller. Hit were rainin' mightily, and he'd been out drivin' some yearlin's up under the clifts, and he felt the yarth tremble and knowed pint-blank he were on a slip, so he throwed his arms around a big sugar-tree, and hilt on. Well, boys, the hull side o' that mountain slid down."

"Trees and all?"

"Yes, sirree, them trees is thar today; they never did stop growin'. Well, Pete come into the house kinder yaller lookin' and sat down by the fire and warmed awhile 'thout sayin' nothin'. Atter awhile he sez, 'I reckon I have rid a bigger critter than ary one of you fellers ever seed.' 'Why, Pete, have you been a-ridin' the elephant at a circus?' 'Naw, sir, hit warn't no elephant. I have rode four acres of land for two hundred yards.'" Such land-slips are no joke. They occur every rainy season. But steep areas are, of course, not thickly settled.

In earlier days a settler would locate at the mouth of a creek. He would first clear the lower levels, then part of the hillsides, not by cutting the trees down, but by belting them. He would notch a six-inch band around the tree and remove the bark therein so that the sap could not go up to nourish the tree. In a few weeks the leaves would wither and the tree die. A field of such trees is called a "deadening." This is the quickest way to make a cornfield. The wood soil, or humus, however, is soon washed away from the hillside, and the field loses its fertility. Whereupon more land is cleared, higher up.

As the sons of a family marry, they must settle higher up the hillsides or farther up the creeks. Thus the creeks determine not only the original routes of travel, but also the trend of population and the development of settlement.

While this Mountain region covers about one third of the area of the nine states mentioned at the head of this chapter, in each of them, except West Virginia, it constitutes such a small part of its state that its population cannot secure legislation suited to their needs. The geographical situation has constantly worked against the Mountain People, making them dependent politically and economically upon majorities who have had no interest in their peculiar problems, whose interests, indeed, have often naturally worked in antagonism.

Adventurers for Freedom

Adventurers for Freedom

BETWEEN the years 1632 and 1750, numerous groups of Pennsylvanians —Germans and Irish largely, with many Quakers among them—had been wending their way through the Mountain troughs and gradually pushing forward the line of settlement, until now it had reached the upper waters of the Yadkin River, in the northwest corner of North Carolina. Trials abundant fell to their lot; but the soil of the valleys was unusually fertile, game was abundant, the climate mild, the country beautiful, and life in general upon the new frontier, although rough, such as to appeal to the borderers as a thing desirable.

REUBEN G. THWAITES
Daniel Boone

CHAPTER THREE

Adventurers for Freedom

THE Mountain People have not a strong sense of history. Even personal traditions are vague. "My foreparents came in through Hurricane Gap, date of four (1804). Where did they come from? Hit were Virginia they moved from, but the McKee generation was Irelandish. I reckon they come from 'cross the water. Granny never knowed whar the Carriers come from." But the history of these people is written into the fabric of America far more indelibly than in their memories. Besides documentary evidence, we have abundant testimony in their family names, their language, their customs, their traditions, their characteristics, and their ballads. All these elements have a Shakespearean flavor and take us back to the "spacious times of Great Elizabeth." Then, Englishmen stimulated by the strong wine of the Renaissance were all eager "to seek beyond the sunset for the Western Isles."

These voyages of romantic exploration and restless adventure opened the way for more sober and permanent efforts. As soon as trading posts were established, large masses of folk who lived under intolerable pressure in various countries turned their thoughts to these new lands as places of refuge from their oppression. By a natural process of selection, successful colonists must be resourceful, powerful, and self-controlled. It is one thing to go into the woods for a week's picnic; it is vastly different to go into the wilderness for the rest of one's life. People who do this must be sustained by a great purpose. This purpose has usually been to achieve freedom, and frequently religious freedom. The Huguenots from France, the Dunkers, Mennonites, and Moravians from Holland and Germany, the Puritans, Quakers, and Catholics from England, together with Scots (especially from the north of Ireland) landed all along the Atlantic coast. They gave up home, property, even civilization, that they might be free.

Political refugees there were also: Cromwellians fleeing from the vengeance of Charles II; Scottish Highlanders loyal to the Stuarts, fleeing from King George; Germans from the Palatine States fleeing from the petty princelings whose voracious taxation would finish the awful desolation of the Thirty Years' War. These, so widely different in race, religion, and social rank, were all seeking freedom, and there was, therefore, in them all an underlying similarity, a strong basis for union. Even those that came for trading and the hope of gain, *if they remained* and established homes, entered into the liberty-loving spirit, and readily coalesced with the other settlers, until they were more or less completely fused with them.

All the early settlers were perforce pioneers;

and in general new settlers, not having property interests or established professional positions, drifted out on the edges of previous settlements to find or make a place for themselves. The more energetic and independent they were, the less likely would they be to become laborers or underlings in projects already under way in the settlements. Thus the most resourceful of the newcomers tended always to settle deeper and deeper in the wilderness. Only such could maintain themselves in the arduous struggle with primitive conditions, hard fare, and the constant danger from forest life and Indians. As a community acquired the comforts and luxuries of urban society, the bolder spirits of the younger generation tended naturally to join the drift to the more adventurous outskirts and become hunters, trappers, and pioneers.

There was thus a continuous movement of population to unoccupied lands on the west, stimulated or retarded by local circumstances—such as Indian attacks, crop shortage, governmental interference, or unusual influx of immigrants. These conditions applied to all the settlements in all the colonies, and must be remembered as the background for the great movement of population that settled the Mountain region.

To understand this sudden and voluminous movement, we must go back to the English invasions of Ireland. Again and again English kings "planted" large numbers of colonists in Ireland after killing or driving out the previous residents. So that "the Irish" in many districts were largely of English blood, and they resented each new invasion with as much vigor and hatred as did their more Celtic neighbors. Queen Elizabeth took her turn in donating Irish lands to courtly favorites if they would "pacify" the districts. This they proceeded to do by war and famine. Three general attempts to "plant" colonists wholesale upon these sequestered lands failed, because the pacified Irish made it too uncomfortable for the newcomers. Shortly after Elizabeth's death, however, James I succeeded in making a "plantation" in Ulster by inducing the hardier, ruggeder, and stubborner Scots to settle there in great numbers. These transplanted Scots are called by American historians Scotch-Irish. In 1610 the land was officially opened for settlers, and permanent communities were soon established. A little later four thousand followed in one emigration, and at the close of the Stuart reigns in 1688 there were fifty thousand Scots in Ulster, and fifty thousand additional families settled there in the two or three years succeeding. But their situation was never comfortable. The dispossessed Irish were hostile, and the English government, after getting the Scots there for its own schemes, instead of assisting them, constantly annoyed them by restrictions and exactions.

One would think that the English government would have favored these Scotch Presbyterians who were their instrument for repressing the uprisings of the Irish Catholics; but the Stuart kings, always besotted with the ambition for autocratic rule, badgered and irritated their Presbyterian "plantations" even more unbearably than they treated the Catholics. No Irish ships were allowed to engage in foreign trade—not even in trade with America. The people were not allowed to worship except in the State churches. The government prohibited them from exporting horses, cattle, or dairy products to England. This selfish and greedy blow followed a generous gift from Ireland of thirty thousand head of cattle towards the relief of London after the Great Fire. As a consequence of this tyrannical legislation, the value of cattle fell fivefold, and horses were worth only one twentieth of what they had been. After years of struggle under these handicaps, Ireland began to thrive on wool. Promptly the English government forbade the export of wool to any country except England, and even to England it could be admitted only under prohibitive duties. Then Ireland tried linen, but as soon as it grew general enough to become profitable, the English government, egged on by the London merchants, killed the linen industry also. The persecution of Presbyterians became more and more severe. They were forbidden to possess arms. They were expelled even from the militia. They were fined incessantly. After paying cess, tithes, and rent, they had left for themselves only about one fourth or one fifth of the results of their labor. If their ministers solemnized marriages, the children were declared illegitimate and could not inherit property.

So they began as early as 1635 to emigrate to America, and after the terrible massacres in 1641 they left in increasing numbers. In 1649 Lord Baltimore offered to give any "adventurer" or "planter" three thousand acres for every thirty persons brought into Maryland. Large numbers of Scotch-Irish thereupon settled there "with free liberty of religion." But Pennsylvania, with its genuine religious liberty and its hearty democratic welcome, soon became the star of hope for the oppressed, and far more Scotch-Irish settled in Pennsylvania than in all the other colonies combined.

To crown all, about 1717, when the leases of most of the farms in County Antrim expired, the rents were doubled and trebled by Lord Donegal. These farms had been waste lands until they were cleared and improved by the unpaid labor of the Scots who settled upon them. To raise three times as much rent money on the lands their own toil had made fertile was financially impossible, even if their indignation had permitted the attempt. Within two years after the Antrim Evictions, thirty thousand more Protestants left Ulster for America. Soon they were sailing at the rate of twelve thousand a year, and by 1774 there were three hundred thousand of them in Pennsylvania alone, and two hundred thousand settled in other parts of America. Fiske estimates that they constituted at that time one sixth of the total population of the colonies.

They found the fertile and accessible lands of Eastern Pennsylvania already occupied. So they traveled farther west, beyond the settlements, and built their cabins in the unbroken forest, each successive emigration going beyond the last, a little farther west. The Penns, as Proprietors, had reserved great tracts of land for themselves, fifteen thousand acres in Conestoga, forty thousand acres at Gettysburg, three hundred thousand sold to English absentees. But the incoming tide of Scotch-Irish could not be held off. Logan, the Secretary of Pennsylvania, writes in 1730 that the Scotch-Irish in an "audacious and disorderly manner" settled upon these tracts, saying it "was against the laws of God and Nature that so much land should be idle while so many Christians wanted it to labor on and to raise their bread." Consequently the Proprietors had to sell it to them, which they did for nominal sums.

It was a racial characteristic that the Scotch-Irish were opposed to paying any rent, however small. Their cruel experience in Ulster had taught them that they might lose all their life's labor on rented land, so they felt at ease only when they owned it themselves. This characteristic persists to this day. A Mountain man recently remarked, "I hain't a-goin' to rent; I'll own some land if hit's only a house-seat." Before the influx of immigrants just mentioned the Scotch-Irish in Pennsylvania had already forced the Proprietors to abolish the system of quit-rents, the annual payment of a few cents an acre (a device of the "Proprietors" to keep a legal hold upon the land). This exemption was not made general, but was granted to the Scotch-Irish on the ground that they formed a barrier and a defense against the Indians.

They were a peaceable folk—many of them having left New England to escape Indian attacks—but when forced to fight, they did it thoroughly, with a ferocity as bloody as that of the Indians, and a stubbornness that finally conquered the enemy. After living a hundred years among the hardships and hostilities of Ulster, nothing could daunt them.

In addition to the great swarms of Scotch-Irish that settled in Pennsylvania, large numbers settled all along the coast, but especially in Maryland and Carolina. Finding here, as elsewhere, the coast lands already occupied, they drifted to the western fringes of settlement. So in the western part of what is now North and South Carolina, in the foothills east of the Blue Ridge, there gathered another large mass of pioneer population, ready later to be drawn into the great stream that flowed down the Valley of Virginia to form the Mountain People.

Nobody knows, of course, when the first settlers entered the beautiful and fertile Shenandoah Valley, which is the first of that chain of delightful upland river bottoms that together form the Valley of Virginia. Alexander Breckinridge from Ulster was comfortably settled there in 1728, though he was swept on later by the migrating flood that finally carried him to Kentucky. About 1732 John Lewis, with his Scottish wife, founded Staunton. This same year a German, or more probably an Alsatian Frenchman from Strassburg, secured a warrant for forty thousand acres for himself and fifteen other families. His name, as spelled by the pioneers, was Joist Hite. These people settled in the Valley near the present site of Winchester, Virginia. Among them were George Bowman, Peter Stephens, Paul Froman (sons-in-law of Joist Hite), Jacob Chrisman, Robert McKay, Robert Green, and William Duff.

During the next few years, encouraged by these beginnings, the migration became a constant and ever-increasing stream. In 1737 we find in Rockbridge County strong settlements of Scotch-Irish, bearing such names as Greenlee, Alexander, Paxton, Lyle, Grigsby, Brown, Matthews, Caruthers,

Telford, Stuart, Crawford, Wilson, Cummins, Campbell, McCampbell, McClung, McKee, and McCuen. Next year each family entering the Valley of Virginia could secure a grant of a thousand acres. By 1740 the Scotch-Irish had settled so thickly around Staunton—the first settler had been there only eight years—that they sent for the Rev. John Craig, who became their settled pastor. And two years later there were enough Germans in the Valley so that itinerant Moravian missionaries made more or less regular visits among them.

The Germans were better farmers than the Scotch-Irish. They were equally thrifty and more practical—for every Scot has a touch of the visionary. The Germans, therefore, acquired the rich, lower-lying limestone lands, cleared the trees out by the roots, and built substantial houses and barns, while the Scotch-Irish, who outnumbered them five to one, pushed up on the hill slopes and farther into the forests to be huntsmen, traders, pioneers, and "settlers," rather than farmers.

The older English settlements in the Seaboard of Virginia had now become so permanent and populous, and life had become so secure and civilized, that they began to hunger for adventure and —good investments. In 1749 the Ohio Company was formed by Thomas Lee, Lawrence and Augustus Washington (brothers of George Washington), and nine or ten other Virginia gentlemen. Their intention was to acquire title to great tracts of land, to send out hunters, trappers, and traders to barter with the Indians and later to sell land to settlers. The scheme promised rich returns. Thirty thousand deerskins were being shipped from North Carolina in a single year, besides the more valuable pelts and furs in unnumbered quantities. The company obtained a charter to locate and settle five hundred thousand acres between the Kanawha and Monongahela Rivers, and upon the waters of the Ohio River below Pittsburgh. They could thus pick their choice from most of West Virginia, Southern Ohio, Southern Indiana, and Northern Kentucky.

They sent out Christopher Gist and a "surveying" party to explore. Three years later George Washington, on his way to confer with the French commander, met Gist at Will's Creek and persuaded him to go with him as guide through the forests.

About the same time Dr. Thomas Walker was doing some very extensive "surveying" for a similar enterprise, the Loyal Land Company, which had a grant of eight hundred thousand acres in what is now Kentucky. His exploring party followed the "warrior's path" down the valley of Virginia, along the Holston River through Tennessee, and over Cumberland Gap into Kentucky, then along the Rockcastle River, up the Kentucky River, across the Big Sandy, and back to Virginia along the Greenbriar River.

Dr. Walker's party consisted of Ambrose Powell, William Tomlinson, Colby Chew, Henry Lawless, and John Hughes. Each had a horse, a rifle, and a dog, while the baggage was carried by two pack horses.

Dr. Walker has left a very interesting and accurate journal of the four months' trip. The last entry in the journal reads, "We killed in the Journey 13 Buffaloes, 8 Elks, 53 Bears, 20 Deer, 4 Wild Geese, about 150 Turkeys, besides small game. We might have killed three times as much meat if we had wanted it."

It should be remembered that hunters often lived almost exclusively upon a meat diet. For weeks they would be without flour or meal. They suffered only if they ran short of salt.

The Indians of western New York, Pennsylvania and Ohio, especially the Shawnees, were very troublesome. They were continually incited by the French, who wished to destroy all English settlements in the Mississippi Valley so that the field might be left clear for French hunters and trappers. But in the early days the Southern Indians, especially the Cherokees, were friendly. They traded with the settlers, sold land to them, and made honorable treaties. Several forts were built with their consent and assistance, and they agreed to furnish specified numbers of warriors to assist the settlers against the French Indians.

The expedition of General Braddock against the

French had important and unforeseen consequences. When the French forces at Fort du Quesne heard of Braddock's approach, they felt already defeated, and their allied Indians naturally shared their dread. But when under Beaujeu's leadership the invincible redcoats were defeated and almost annihilated by mere Indians, respect for the white man's warfare gave way to a self-confident eagerness for revenge against all these English-speaking settlers that had invaded their hunting-grounds. Attacks on the settlements became frequent. In 1762 the Indians killed or captured two thousand persons and drove two thousand families from their homes on Pennsylvania's western border. At Muddy Creek sixty Indians visited the settlement as friends and were treated hospitably, but they murdered all the men and marched the women and children through the forest until they approached another settlement. There the Indians left the women under guard outside the settlement while they went inside and effected another treacherous massacre and capture. The frontier settlers made vigorous appeals for help to the Pennsylvania Assembly, but the Assembly paid no heed. What did it matter if a lot of these headstrong Scotch-Irish were massacred? To emphasize their plea, the frontiersmen even drove a wagon-load of the corpses through the streets of Philadelphia; but the Assembly offered neither help nor sympathy; and they sent neither soldiers nor ammunition. No wonder, as Parkman records, "The frontier people of Pennsylvania, goaded to desperation by long-continued suffering, were divided between rage against the Indians and resentment against the Quakers who had yielded them cold sympathy and inefficient aid."

The Scotch-Irish thereupon organized several companies of Rangers to defend the settlements, and fighting with Indians gradually became more common than friendship with them.

The failure of the Assembly to send help in defense of the outlying settlements resulted in a great petition sent by a strong deputation to Philadelphia to demand for the frontier people a greater share in the government of Pennsylvania.

The activity of the Indians and the inactivity of the Pennsylvanian government combined to stimulate the immigration of the frontier people down the Valley of Virginia, which was soon dotted farther and farther with settlers' cabins, and in 1764 two townships, Mecklenburg and Londonderry, were laid out in North Carolina.

Always as the settlers pushed farther on, the fringe of hunters and trappers took flight and moved before them farther into the depths of the wilderness. But while they hurried on to escape from the forest clearing of the settlers, they really formed the entering wedge for the forces of civilization that followed them.

We have now noted three reasons why migration moved down the Valley of Virginia instead of moving west from New York, Pennsylvania, and Virginia, across the Alleghenies: (1) the rough, jagged, impenetrable surface of the mountains on the west; (2) the rich soil, the scenery, and the delightful hunting found in the Valley itself; (3) the hostile Indians on the west and the consequent proclamation of the authorities forbidding settlers to go on the other side of the Mountains.

Yet, in spite of these excellent reasons, men went west. Before Braddock's defeat, Christopher Gist had spent a couple of years exploring and hunting on the Ohio River and some of its tributaries, notably the Scioto, the Miami, the Licking, and the Kentucky. John Findlay went in a canoe down the Ohio as far as the site of Louisville, and thence with the Shawnees he tramped through the wilderness to Kan-ta-ke, an Indian corn granary, perhaps a dozen miles east of the present town of Winchester, Kentucky.

All such exploring parties consisted of about half a dozen well-armed, experienced woodsmen. After these organized scouting expeditions, hunters and trappers naturally followed by ones or twos. They were men who lived alone all winter in a rough shack while they killed enormous quantities of fur-bearing animals and deer. As more and more hunters were attracted by the reports of hides being brought out, the game grew scarcer, and some of the hunters brought their families and settled down as semi-farmers, while the rest moved deeper into the forest.

Perhaps we can perceive this wave-like, or pendulum, progress of hunters and settlers if we follow the migrations of a typical family, such as were the Boones, the Lincolns, the Seviers, or the Robertsons.

In 1750 Daniel Boone moved with his father, brothers, and uncles from their home in Pennsylvania into the Valley of Virginia. They stayed in Rockingham County one season, presumably to raise a crop of corn. They then moved on down to the valley of the river Yadkin. Here the father and most of the uncles settled permanently and lived the rest of their lives. But Daniel, fifteen or sixteen years after his marriage, moved his family to Watauga, in Tennessee, a region he had explored ten or twelve years before. He had scarcely built his cabin before the whole valley was overrun with Scotch-Irish from North Carolina, coming there by thousands on account of the wrongs they received from the Government officials.

The next year, accordingly, in 1773, Daniel Boone and his wife, Rebecca Bryan, and their children started for Kentucky, where Boone had been hunting and exploring some years before. With them went forty Bryans, Captain William Russell, and several others. But in Powell's Valley, just before they reached Cumberland Gap, the mountain pass into Kentucky, they were attacked by Indians. Several were killed, among them Boone's eldest son, and the party decided to return to Watauga until the region became safer. Boone, having already sold his Watauga home, went into the Clinch Valley, near Russell. Two years later he moved his family to Boonesboro, where, in the meantime, he had built log cabins and started a stockade or fort. His migration from Pennsylvania, where he had lived sixteen years, to Kentucky thus took twenty-five years. He spent a year in Virginia, twenty years in four different places in North Carolina, and four years in Tennessee.

It was, therefore, when he was forty-one years old, that he thus brought his family to Boonesboro, and he lived in Kentucky thirteen years. Then Boone's land was seized on technical error by shrewd title-sharks, and in 1788 he moved to the mouth of the Great Kanawha River, now in West Virginia. For eleven years he lived hereabout, but again coming into conflict with registered titles, in 1799 he decided to go beyond the jurisdiction of the United States. Accordingly, he moved across the Mississippi River into Spanish territory, penetrating nearly fifty miles west of St. Louis, and here lived for twenty years. His wife died when he was seventy-eight, and shortly thereafter he was persuaded to give up living alone in his cabin. From that time he lived in his son's two-story stone house. Yet in his eighty-fifth year his sons could scarcely restrain him from starting out alone, or with an Indian lad, to begin life anew in the unexplored Rocky Mountains.

Boone always felt uncomfortably restricted when neighbors crowded their homes too close around him. He wanted to live in the open. He enjoyed the freedom of the unfenced wilderness. His life therefore was a succession of flights from his neighbors. However, he was not a recluse. In fact he was very genial and social in his nature, always enjoying neighbors—but not too close. He wanted elbow room. Like a sociable English gentleman, he needed a scope of land large enough to be alone when he wished. In this Boone was typical; he constantly led settlers into new territory, and as constantly fled from their midst as soon as they began to clear the forests.

The settlements on the Watauga are historically important, and we can get a glimpse of their development and at the same time note another instance of the wave-like progress of the settlers if we follow the migrations of the Robertson family.

In 1760 Daniel Boone and others had hunted through the region, and, as was usually the case, the first settlers followed the first hunters eight or ten years later. Accordingly, in 1768 we find a few settlers in the Watauga Valley.

James Robertson, a Scotch-Irishman who had settled in Orange County, North Carolina, was much dissatisfied with the political and social conditions in that locality. The older parts of North Carolina had been settled long enough to develop an aristocracy composed of the prosperous and influential people. They controlled the Assembly and the Government and made laws to suit themselves, as aristocracies always do. They looked down upon the swarm of new immigrants that was sweeping along the Valley of Virginia into the rugged western end of Carolina. Corrupt officials, sheriffs, taxgatherers, even judges, raised in the pioneers a storm of angry protest. When the protest was unheeded, the Mountain men, burning with a sense of injustice and insult, organized themselves into armed bands called Regulators, whose purpose was to see justice done by the courts. But there is always danger that such bands may be too hasty in resenting wrongs. Some of the more thoughtful and steady citizens discussed the wisdom of moving away from Carolina into the wilderness that was under the rule of Virginia, the government of which they considered less corrupt.

James Robertson volunteered to go on an exploring expedition. In the valley of the Watauga he found two settlers, William Bean, doubtless of Scottish Highland blood, and a man named Honeycut. Robertson liked the region and staked out land for himself and friends. He stayed at Honeycut's cabin while he cleared some land and raised a crop of corn. After gathering his corn, he left it in Honeycut's care and returned for his family and neighbors. During his year of absence the situation in Carolina had grown from bad to worse. The officials had become more insolent, the Regulators more determined, until a battle had been fought, May 16, 1771. Governor Tryon, instead of investigating the charges of corruption and injustice, had marched into the disaffected district with a thousand of the militia. The Mountain People, hearing of his coming, gathered with their rifles at Alamance, two thousand of them, and, demanding justice, refused to disperse. The battle lasted all day. The Regulators, having no supply of ammunition, were finally forced to withdraw, leaving two hundred of their number dead on the field. Robertson's glowing report of Watauga, coming in such a time of gloom, was decisive with his neighbors, and sixteen families started at once for the new lands staked out for them in the western reaches of Virginia.

But they were soon disappointed to learn that the new survey of the western borders—necessitated by recent Indian treaties—left the Watauga region outside of both Virginia and Carolina. Robertson and his neighbors therefore made a treaty with the Indian tribe and leased from them the land he had staked out. Some of the settlers

A WINDOWLESS CABIN

A young fellow marries a girl and builds a one-room house—often windowless—with a chimney built of thin strips of wood laid up crosswise and plastered inside and out with clay. If the young people are healthy and thrifty, they will soon add to their house, or replace it by a better.

WHERE RIVERS AND STREAMS ABOUND

In the beautiful "Valley of Virginia" a traveler, as in old romance, hails the ferryman from the opposite shore. With a large oar or pole the owner propels his boat in the path allowed it by a wire cable to which it is attached by a ring. Beside another Mountain stream is a natural fall. Here another traveler hails the miller, who with a twelve- or fifteen-foot wheel grinds his "turn" of corn into "bread."

seem to have bought land from individual Indians, an unusual proceeding.

As soon as these seventeen families were settled, thousands followed them from their old home. They were outside the boundaries of civilized government, therefore the leading men bound themselves into an association, drew up a constitution, and established the first republic in America. Theodore Roosevelt in *The Winning of the West* admits that this constitution was "the first ever adopted by a community of American born freemen."

It is interesting to note the contribution made by the Mountain People to the idea of independence and the spirit of democracy. General historical statements can be at best only approximate. Many Scotch-Irish that did not go into the Mountains eagerly joined, both in thinking and in action, with their bolder and more direct kinsfolk of the frontier. Hanna says, "It was Patrick Henry and his Scotch-Irish brethren from the western counties that carried and held Virginia for independence."

In the colonies there were many partisans of the King who did all they could to prevent the movement for Independence. Outside of New England about one third of the population were Tories. There were no Tories among the Scotch-Irish. Their experiences with the royal government for two hundred years had been too severe. Bitter injustice, humiliating insults, cruel taxation, hypocritical ecclesiastical exactions, religious persecution, and supercilious oppression had hammered their resistance into steel. Their minds and memories were too keen for smooth words to deceive them. "The active part which the Scotch-Irish took in the American Revolution was a continuation of popular resistance to British policy that began in Ulster."[1]

Because they lived far in the wilderness, with no protection from the settlements or government officials, they learned to protect themselves. This habit of self-reliance, of personal independence, added to their resentment at British aggression, made them inevitably resisters of tyranny. And their remoteness from polite society, together with their Scottish bluntness, made them assert their determination with unmistakable clearness and force. Such men, expressing vigorously their positive convictions, strongly influenced the whole community and naturally became leaders of thought and action. The Palatine Germans, the Dutch and the French Huguenots, with similar background of persecution, easily followed their lead.

The English settlers also that seeped into the Mountain population from Virginia had inherited traditions of prompt and resolute action that

[1] Ford, *The Scotch-Irish in America*, p. 458.

readily fused into the frontier spirit of independence.

If we were not so ignorant of the history of the Mountain People, it would not surprise us that they took such leadership in the movement for American Independence. The declaration and constitution of the Watauga Association in 1772; the declaration at Abingdon, Virginia, in January, 1775; the raising of the flag of a new and independent nation called Transylvania at Boonesboro, Kentucky, May 23, 1775; the Mecklenburg Resolutions in North Carolina, May 31, 1775; all these declarations by Mountain men made possible the more widespread Continental Declaration of Independence at Philadelphia, July 4, 1776.

The large population of Scotch-Irish scattered throughout all the colonies had not yet been absorbed by the older population and settled into conventional compliance. When Independence was being agitated, they naturally followed the fearless lead of their frontier brethren and thus gave unity to the whole movement.

The Atlantic settlements were isolated from each other by virtue of their geographic position, but they were isolated even more because of differences in feeling. The Puritans of New England were very different from the Dutch of New York, and they were also very different from the English in Virginia. The Scotch-Irish, on the other hand, were one people, united by mood and feeling, in spite of the fact that they were scattered throughout New England, New York, Pennsylvania, Maryland, Virginia, and all the Carolinas. And it was just because all the Scotch-Irish felt and behaved the same way no matter where they lived that their widespread settlement actively leavened their different communities and made possible an organized unity of feeling and purpose that was continental in its scope.

Even so brief an historical sketch as this would be incomplete without some consideration of the large share the Mountain People had in fighting for Independence—as well as in talking for it.

George Washington led a company of these Mountain men against the French in 1754, but was driven back at Great Meadows. The following year when General Braddock came to punish the French for their insolence Washington accompanied him with a hundred Mountain men from North Carolina, young Daniel Boone being among them. All through the French and Indian War, the defence of the western settlements was left to the Mountain men, and they supplied besides many experienced Indian fighters for the armies that fought on the Northern border and invaded Canada.

As soon as the Continental Congress had launched the Revolution by appointing Washington commander, the first troops to join him were Mountain men—Morgan's Riflemen and Nelson's

Riflemen. Washington had led these frontiersmen before, and he welcomed them gladly at Cambridge. They brought with them, of course, their own hunting rifles, and thus were the first to use rifles in warfare. They were of great service to Washington, not only on account of their skill as sharpshooters, but because of their cool courage and determination. They were men who could be trusted to act alone with fearless judgment. It was their quality of personal independence that won the battles of King's Mountain and Cowpens and drove Lord Cornwallis to his surrender at Yorktown.

The Mountain men were keenly aware of Ferguson's published threat to hang them and destroy their homes. When they heard of his march towards the frontier settlements with eleven hundred well-equipped soldiers, they gathered by scores at Isaac Shelby's summons, and a thousand met at the Sycamore Shoals of the Watauga River.

They pushed on through the snow-encumbered forests very rapidly, some on horses and some on foot, scarcely stopping to eat or sleep until they reached Cowpens the night of October sixth. Here they had expected to find the enemy. But Ferguson had adroitly slipped away.

Several hundred fresh men joined them here, bringing news of the British encampment thirty miles away. They slaughtered a few cattle, swallowed some hastily cooked beef, and in less than an hour all that had fit horses—perhaps seven hundred and fifty—hurried on. Many eagerly followed on foot. They marched all night in the rain, and reached King's Mountain, on the top of which were the British, about three o'clock in the morning. It was a long mound sloping up on three sides, but a sheer precipice on the fourth. Without waiting to rest or eat, the frontiersmen attacked Ferguson's soldiers, entrenched behind baggage wagons on the top of this mound. Isaac Shelby had told the Mountain men to shelter themselves as much as possible behind trees and rocks; to aim carefully; and to "get" the British. His final instruction was "Every man must be his own officer, and use his own judgment."

The British commander and 224 of his soldiers were killed, 163 were wounded, and 716 surrendered as prisoners. Of the Mountain men 28 were killed and 68 were wounded. This surprising victory turned back Cornwallis' expedition, and was the first step in his defeat.

Daniel Morgan with his riflemen struck another astonishing blow at Cowpens the next year (December 17, 1781), when he routed Tarleton, who lost 110 killed, 258 severely wounded, and 600 prisoners. The rest fled. A British writer says that "during the whole period of the war, no other action reflected so much dishonor on the British arms."

In the War of 1812 a large proportion of the

land forces were men from the Mountain region. In a report to the United States Senate in 1834, the committee mentions five hundred pensioners of the Revolutionary War that were even then living in the mountains of Kentucky. The rest of Appalachia could undoubtedly have shown as great a proportion. In the Civil War the Mountain People were overwhelmingly on the side of the Union, and furnished far more than their quota of fighters.

With such noble history in mind, it would seem scarcely necessary to notice an erroneous statement made long ago by a careless writer, but it has been so widely quoted that a brief reference to the facts must be made to correct it. This statement maintains that the Mountain People took their origin from Indents, Redemptioners, and Convicts. As a matter of fact, very few of the convicts deported to America had committed gross criminal offenses. Most of them were victims of religious or political persecution merely and should under no circumstances be identified with the low criminal class. So far from being criminals in the ordinary sense, they were sometimes of the noblest blood and the highest moral excellence. Moreover, the total number of convicts sent to the Virginias by English judges was very small. They would not constitute one thousandth part of the progenitors of the Mountain People, even if they had all left the settlements and gone into the mountains. There is little evidence that any of them ever left the seaboard settlements.

Indents were persons bound by written agreements (indentures) to work for a specified number of years. Their labor was sold so that for the time specified they were virtually slaves. Because they were free after the specified time they were often called Redemptioners. The sale of Redemptioners was not abolished until 1820.

The whole system was largely a scheme of the ship owners. Some of them paid emigration agents three florins for every person over ten years old whom they induced to embark. These agents, pretending to be friends, fleeced the emigrants. In many instances, with the connivance of the ship owners, the passengers' baggage and food supplies for the voyage were not put on board, then exorbitant sums were charged for food, and the betrayed passengers were forced to sign an agreement to sell their labor for several years to pay their passage. To mention a few cases:

(1) A noble lady banked one thousand rixthalers with one of these agents, who stole it, and she, with her two half-grown daughters and a young son, was sold in 1753.

(2) John Reinier, who was abundantly supplied, was robbed by the ship-captain of money, books, and drugs, and was forced to sell himself for seven years.

(3) Fred Helfenstein, probably a lineal de-

scendant of the Emperor Maximilian, similarly was forced to sell himself as a Redemptioner in Georgia.

(4) Abraham Gale of Maryland sent for his wife and two sons. They sailed from Dublin, but fell in with a rascal who sold them ostensibly to pay passage, although Gale stood ready to pay it over again.

Instances of this sort indicate that being a Redemptioner was not necessarily a disgrace. But while such victims were far too numerous, only the grossest ignorance could imagine that the five millions of our Mountain People could have sprung from so small a source. Besides this, the Redemptioners were obviously not free to go out to the frontier, and most of them, after their servitude was ended, naturally became part of the seaboard population where they were. It is evident that very few of these "bound out" persons could ever have penetrated into the mountains, certainly not in numbers large enough to have any perceptible influence either for good or for evil upon the Mountain People.

In these days of somewhat formidable and diverse programs of Americanization, it is well to spend a little time surveying our origin. What were the purposes, human or divine, that gave birth to our nation? What were the elements selected from the Old World out of which to build the New?

The symbol of America is the pioneer, hardy, honest, independent, fearless. At the heart of our nation are the simple virtues of the frontier. The true spirit of America is the pioneer spirit. The history of America is a series of pioneerings, each successive frontier pushed farther into the wilderness than the last.

The ideal American must have the hunger for liberty and the practical courage that impelled our fathers to cross the uncharted ocean and brave the rigors of the wilderness alone. He must also rise above the allurement of personal comfort. He must be indifferent to the affectation of aristocracy or social superiority. He must be cautious, yet friendly. He must think for himself, yet be hospitable to new ideas. He must be democratic, yet never swept away by the mob. He must have in his heart's core a trust in God, a reverence for woman, a loyalty to the family, yet his most serious thoughts are lit up by a sense of humor that insists on setting things in their true proportion.

In the recesses of the Appalachian Mountains these fundamental elements of the American character are found today in stark simplicity, uncontaminated by the rush of business or the greed of money; unencrusted with social ambitions; unbroken by industrial fears. This rich deposit of true Americanism is a priceless possession, the unspoiled heritage of the American people.

Elizabethan Virtues

Elizabethan Virtues

IF the question were submitted to an impartial jury as to what is the chief trait of Highland people the world over, the answer would be independence. Should one ask the outstanding trait manifested by the pioneer, the reply would be independence. Inquire what is the characteristic trait of rural folk, particularly of the farming class, and independence will again be the answer. Put the query as to what is the prevailing trait of the American, and the unanimous verdict is likely to be independence. We have then, in the Southern Highlander, an American, a rural dweller of the agricultural class, and a mountaineer who is still more or less of a pioneer. His dominant trait is independence raised to the fourth power.

JOHN C. CAMPBELL
*The Southern Highlander
and His Homeland*

CHAPTER FOUR

Elizabethan Virtues

IT is perhaps inevitable, but none the less unfortunate, that most of those who write about the Mountain People do not live among them. It is very easy to portray oddities instead of fundamental and vital traits. The outsider naturally notices peculiarities and describes them. These are thereupon taken to be representative, when they may be decidedly exceptional. This does not mean that we should expect everyone to agree with our own observations. It is doubtless true that if a thousand outsiders who had observed Mountain People and Mountain conditions for over a year should be consulted, they might not be at all unanimous about the dominant characteristics of the Mountain People.

Some observers say that there are no *racial* characteristics. They insist that such peculiarities as they have are merely local, that any body of people shut apart for two hundred years among mountains and narrow valleys would necessarily take on the exact idiosyncrasies here found. These observers have perhaps an unnecessary timidity about the word racial, as if any differences that could be called racial would be a stamp of inferiority. But is it true that any and every strain of humanity is necessarily inferior to the conglomerate mixture of our American population?

Other observers describe them as so distinct from the rest of us that we can scarcely feel much kinship with them. Their actions, their motives, their outlook upon life, are portrayed as so different from ours that they are made to seem a strange, peculiar, and far-off people.

Both of these views are extreme and are therefore erroneous. Each ignores very important aspects of the matter. There can be no doubt after careful consideration that the geographical factors of the country have had tremendous influence on the Mountain People. The rural problem which confronts us in all parts of the country is here very strongly accentuated. As everywhere else, it is roughly measured by the distance of the rural community from its agora. This agora must signify a place not merely for buying and selling, but for the exchange of thought as well. It is a forum as well as a market-place. It is the heart and center of communal life. Here is the nucleus of transportation, education, legislation, religion, and recreation.

Since the distance of a rural community from its agora is estimated, not in miles, but in the time and effort of travel, a mountain community with no real roads is the most rural of all; it is rural almost to isolation. Life in such a community is limited by very serious deprivations. But life here also develops great qualities of resourcefulness, independence, and leisure, such as can hardly be gained in city life.

These forces of environment, however strong their impress, are not sufficient to account for the Mountain People. They possessed remarkable qualities inherent in themselves before ever they came into this environment. It is, of course, not quite accurate to speak of the characteristics common to them as racial, since the Mountain People are not all from one race or nationality. Broadly speaking, however, they constitute a race, built up out of like-minded folk from among the English, French, Germans, and Scotch-Irish.

They were a peculiar people when they came to America, and their peculiarities have curiously survived, in spite of the weathering of time. The settlement of America was due primarily to the hunger for freedom and the tremendous enthusiasms awakened by the Renaissance. Elizabethan England was a nation of young life that had just found its strength. It was the spirit of youth just entering maturity and enjoying its new-found powers. Naturally it was a time of tremendous energy and daring, when a people leaped from childhood into manhood. Tingling with the verve of the unbounded currents of new life, they launched with passionate eagerness into every new channel that lay open. Venturesome and self-confident, they explored the uncharted seas in tiny ships. With similar dash and delight, they pushed into the unexplored regions of knowledge, until the universities moldering with a few priests and monks became crowded with men eager for learning, hungry for the new-born science.

All the interests of life were bathed in the golden glow of a magnificent imagination. Their new-kindled enthusiasm expressed itself in manifold activities. The same man was soldier and sailor, explorer and merchant, scholar and courtier, statesman and poet. It was these men, and the sons of such—men of unconquerable energy and unclouded hope—that dared to face the storms of the Atlantic and conquer a new world. What was true of Elizabethan England, was, in a lesser degree, true of all these other countries that had felt the eager stirrings of the Renaissance. In the majority of the migrations, the core of this freedom was a religious conviction. The heart of this resolute spirit of personal independence was, in the leaders, a personal loyalty to God.

Their sense of citizenship was unusually strong. They refused to be serfs or peasants; they were conscious of being men, men with serious self-respect and unbounded determination. They dared to assert individual rights. The rights they cared most about were the rights of conscience, the right to worship God as their enlightened consciences directed. These men, then, with this hunger for freedom, this personal loyalty to God, this abounding joy in the life of the unspoiled out-of-doors,

QUILTS AND "KIVERS"

"On bright summer days Aunt Sally brings out her store of 'bed kivers' and 'kiverlids' and hangs them on the 'gyarden pickets' to 'sun out the moth eggs.'" Sometimes in geometrical patterns, sometimes in floral designs, vari-colored pieces of coth are sewed upon white backgrounds, to make quilts. "Kivers" or "coverlids" are woven from homespun wool dyed in home-made decoctions. The patterns shown in the lower picture are (from left ot right) Snail-trail, Chariot Wheel, Double Chariot Wheel, and (below) Federal City, Virginia Beauty, Lee's Surrender, and Blooming Leaf.

COOPERATION AND COMPENSATION

"We allers make our sweetnin' from a sugar-tree, or raise a patch o' sorghum." The whole family joins both in making molasses and in drying fruit, layer by layer. Usually the "woman" super-intends these operations.

were already a peculiar people. The Nonconformists from England, the Scotch from North Ireland, the Protesters from Germany, the Huguenots from France, were all loyal to a personal conviction and indignant at a personal tyranny. The achievement of independence of conduct against such obstacles demanded strong individualism, a trait made even stronger by the struggle. Added to this, the pioneer life of the new world developed still further their Elizabethan characteristics of determined independence, personal resourcefulness, and untamable youth. The pioneers were eager to know life in all its height and depth, its breadth and richness.

Their personal independence, springing from a passionate love of freedom, developed in them and in their descendants an unusual resourcefulness, an ability to get things, in some rough fashion, accomplished. They acquired a mastery over the forces of nature sufficient for their immediate purpose. While this did not give technical efficiency, it did promote personal initiative. It did not invent machinery, but it did develop resourceful men.

The quiet courage of the pioneer faces as part of the day's work the dangers of the woods: wild animals, tree-limbs broken off by a storm, the torrent of water during a tide in the creek that carries everything in the narrow valley before it; landslides after long rains have softened the whole side of a mountain; or quicksands in the fords of the river. He is used to going into all these dangers alone. He does not depend on his neighbors for help; he expects to manage somehow by himself. This quiet confidence in meeting emergencies, this habit of self-sufficiency, does not fit the Mountain man for gregarious enterprises. He is rather suspicious of cooperation. A man who asks a neighbor to help him undertake some task that every man usually does for himself must be lazy or incompetent—or "afeard." Such a man will bear watching. Some such suspicious mood as this is back of the Mountain man's slowness to cooperate.

Then there is the Mountaineer's lack of enthusiasm for work, as such, and his strongly developed love of leisure. He has inherited the Calvinistic vividness of the primal curse which laid work upon man, not as a delight or a means to joyful achievement, but as a stark penalty, a doom to be escaped whenever possible. If one is fastidious, querulous about comforts, dissatisfied unless he has this and that, of course he must spend laborious days to procure these coveted things. But if one is satisfied with Nature's own providing and finds unalloyed pleasure where the Naiads of the streams and the Nymphs of the forest have never been disturbed, why reproach him for indulging in philosophic and contemplative leisure?

In the complicated civilization of modern life

we have standardized everything. There are no longer any individualities. Our family breakfasts are standardized. We all eat the same patent cereal and the same brand of bacon. We all have similar twin-beds and similar bathtubs. We wear the same undergarments and the same collars. The Mountain People, however, have not reached this stage. Being strong individualists, they take no pains to subdue their personal preferences in order to agree with what the social majority has declared proper. A Mountain man is not ashamed to avow his dislike of coffee or grapenuts, asparagus or soup. "I'm obleeged to you, I wouldn't choose," settles the matter without any explanatory apologies. He has never adopted the slogan of the mob, "Let's make it unanimous!"

Living mostly out of doors, with no very near neighbors, and with this strongly developed tendency toward personal freedom, we can scarcely expect him to have a highly developed social consciousness, a trained sense of civic solidarity.

On the other hand, the unconquerable and unquenchable spirit of youth, the zest for new experiences, the joy in exploring in spite of hardships, have produced a poise of mind and an ease of manner that are a constantly refreshing surprise. For Mountain People life has a zest which does not depend upon comforts. They are nature lovers, and they take Nature as they find her, without interjecting so many complicated conveniences.

This love of nature does not express itself in songs or poems about the woods, the flowers, or the sky. It is not a matter of words. The Highlanders' delight in it is largely inarticulate. Their joy is not in describing their contact with Nature, but in the contact itself, in feeling Nature's soothing touch upon them, in the things they can do out of doors. "Uncle Bog Stallins," an old pioneer still living "back in some purty rough country," illustrates the essential boyishness of their out-of-door ambitions.

"Do you know Mr. Stallins?" a Mountaineer was asked.

"Uncle Bog Stallins! Why, this creek were named for him. He's been right puny this winter, but he's peart. He had killed ninety-nine bar in his lifetime, and war fixin' fer another hunt, when he tuk sick with a misery in his stummick. The doctors told him he'd got to die. But he prayed the good Lord to raise him up to kill jest one more bar, and shore enough He done it."

How faint and far-off seem the usual ambitions of life from the quaint seclusion of Uncle Bog's world, with its far-stretching forest filled with timber, game, and all that a man needs if he but attune his life to the simple chords of the forest harmonies.

The Mountain men today are called shiftless because they do not flock to the city where they might enjoy the great benefit of crowds, confusion, and noise. They prefer grass and wild flowers or the rustle of leaves to pavements. They get more satisfaction from a hilltop view than from sky scrapers and factory smoke. They enjoy hunting more than golf. Must they, therefore, be called uncivilized? Even "civilized" people spend vacations hunting or fishing. They forego the intricate and expensive conveniences of their homes. They sleep outdoors on a blanket; smoke their eyes out cooking their own food on a camp fire; go wet and dirty, and seem to enjoy their three weeks' reversion to savagery. Why? Presumably because it is outdoors, and they feel the recuperative and satisfying contact with Nature. The Mountain People want this satisfaction to be constant and are willing to forego the city's elaborate comforts in order to live closer to Nature's breast. They are still tent-dwellers by preference.

Besides the confident personal resourcefulness and the adventurous and picnicking spirit of youth, there is a third fundamental trait—neighborliness. This also is a pioneer virtue. In the wilderness a traveler's need constitutes a strong claim, but added to that is the fact that it is a pleasure to see a stranger. A host feels well repaid when he gives food and shelter to a man that brings news from afar. If the traveler be also a pioneer, there is a frankness on both sides, a sort of family familiarity; their intercourse is easy, humanly friendly. The host has only a verbal and conventional apology for the meagerness of his fare. What is good enough for him is good enough for anybody. He offers it without embarrassment. He meets you as an undoubted equal, unabashed and unafraid.

Anything that might seem inhospitable is simply unthinkable. A sister-in-law with a shiftless husband and half a dozen children descends without invitation and almost without warning upon a family whose house has two rooms and a lean-to shed for cooking. The family "have mighty leetle to do with." It is a hard struggle to provide for their own little brood. They live sparely and handle very little money in the course of the year, but they welcome her without comment. They divide up the bedding and make shake-up beds upon the floor every night. They sell their hog—their sole hope for the winter's meat and lard—to buy groceries and meat, as week follows week. They use up most of their canned fruit. But they never hint that the visit is unduly prolonged.

The Mountain man is reticent and inclined to be shy or suspicious with strangers, but this seldom interferes with his hospitality. His house, his food, his furniture, often seem meager, yet, if you, an utter stranger, were to appear unexpectedly at the door, he would welcome you with a simple and sincere, "We're pore folks, we hain't got much, but you're welcome to what we have." We might not consider his home sufficiently provisioned to dispense a generous hospitality. But he never hesitates. He has acquired much skill and experience in doing without. When all "brought-on" purchases must be carried on horseback in saddle-bags, there will occasionally be a scarcity of lamp-chimneys, baking powder, chinaware, or wheat flour. Dress-goods chosen and bought by the men on their journeys to the county seat are not likely to contribute to the beauty of the home.

The Mountain People are essentially honest. They are, as a rule, shrewd and enjoy a bargain. They are likely to emphasize the good points of the horse or cow they want to sell or swap. Trading is a game which two are supposed to play. But they are fundamentally honest. I have lived ten years without any locks on the doors, most of the time without a dog to guard the house, yet nothing has been stolen from it.

The Mountain man is religious, if not always in practice, at least in unspoken reverence for God, the Bible, and the ordinances of religion. Scoffers are rare. Their philosophy is more proverbial than speculative, the wisdom of conduct, rather than a hungry-hearted search for origins. There is, as might be expected, a shy strain of a literalized mysticism occasionally apparent. A man once asked me if I had considered what would have happened if Abraham had slain Isaac before the interrupting angel showed him the thicket-caught ram. "Well, Jesus wouldn't never have come onto the yearth. Kase we'd have been saved by the blood of Isaac.'' I will confess that this proposition gave me quite a shock and opened no mental thoroughfare. ''The Bible says salvation's by the shedding of blood, and hit war to come through Abraham's seed, warn't it? Well, if he'd shed Isaac's blood, ye see salvation would ha' come through Isaac, wouldn't it? And thar 'ud never been no need fer Jesus, then.'' Whatever queer turns Biblical interpretation may take, there is seldom any disposition to question the authority of the Bible. Scripture is an impregnable rock, whose commands admittedly ought to be obeyed. But a failure to obey is considered a transgression much less flagrant than a defiant rejection or denial of the Bible's authority.

The other extreme, superstition, is more uncommon. But here and there an octogenarian believes in witchcraft and the laying of spells.

''Old Doc was a-walkin' along with his wife. They was both elderly. She said, 'Let's go up to this house and git a light for our pipes.' (Folks didn't have matches—none to speak of—in them days; many a time I've walked a mile to a neighbor's with a shovel to borrow fire.) Well, they found a child thar screamin' and kickin'—bewitched. Doc told 'em to git him nine new pins that hadn't never been stuck in cloth and a bottle. He putt the pins in the bottle and set it on the fireboard (mantel-shelf). Then he got a shingle and drew a picture of a witch-woman and told the man to set it up agin a stump and shoot it jest at sundown. About a week atter that, Doc was comin' by agin, and he inquired atter the child. Hit were all right. Then he axed had anybody died suddintly, and they told him an old woman across the valley had died with a shriek, ever when the man shot the picture with his rifle-gun. And the bottle on the fireboard busted into a thousand pieces, and they never did find ary one of the pins."

When ordinary means fail, a Mountaineer may consult a witch-doctor instead of an agricultural expert when "the cow gives quar milk, and the butter won't come." But his habit of doing things for himself instead of calling for help, together with his innate resourcefulness, largely counteracts fantastic notions.

A visit to Uncle Abner and Aunt Sally, up on the headwaters of Rock Creek where no wagon has ever been, may give us a picture of the simple life that is not merely a philosophic pose. He and Aunt Sally have had eighteen children, all of whom are living. They have all left home except one young man, who "farms it" on the old place, and takes care of the old people. Aunt Sally is large, active, and well preserved. She mounts a mule and rides a dozen miles to the store. She has a few sheep, whose wool she cards and spins into yarn. Then she dyes it, warps it, and weaves it on the heavy loom that her grandsire made mostly with his ax. "Hit ain't so purty as the fotch-on goods, but it's a heap endurabler. When my gals was a-raisin', afore they married off, I allers aimed to git 'em some store clothes, and not shame 'em none afore the fellers. But fur us old folks, homespun air good a-plenty."

On bright summer days, Aunt Sally brings out her store of "bed kivers" and "kiverlids" and hangs them on the "gyarden pickets" (the split paling fence) to "sun out the moth eggs." The "kivers" are woven in pretty designs, blue and white, or white and red—"mather red"—madder being one of the most desirable dyes. Or the dye may be brown, made from the hulls of black walnuts, or brownish yellow, from hickory bark. Besides these "wool kivers," she exhibits with pride half a dozen coverlids with roses, lilies, and sunflowers cut out of various colored cloth and sewed upon a white background.

She has no kitchen stove because Uncle Abner thinks victuals taste better when cooked at the fireplace. "Come in and set awhile, and I'll make some gritted bread for supper. Don't ye love gritted bread with honey?" Aunt Sally brings in a board with a gigantic nutmeg grater on it, on which she rubs a dozen ears of milky corn. From the grated pulp she bakes the most delicious "gritted bread." "I allers keep a stand o' honey; hit's the healthiest sweetenin' ther is."

"What's a *stand*, Aunt Sally?"

"Why, hit's this," pointing to what looks like an enormous wooden churn that would hold about fifteen gallons.

"What is it made of?"

"Hit's made from mulberry staves, and the hoops is hickory. My grandmother had it when she were married."

Uncle Abner shows us a corn mill that he turns by hand. It consists of two round stones set in the top of a short, upright gum log. The top stone has a hole in the center through which he pours the corn with one hand while he turns the stone with the other.

"Isn't that pretty slow work, Uncle Abner?"

"Well, the old mortars were a heap tediouser. Folks usen to burn out a sort of bowl in a tree stump and then scrape it clean. Then they'd bend over a little hickory tree near by and tie the pestle to hit's top. They'd pull down the pestle and pound the corn in the mortar, and the hickory would spring it up again, ready to pound down again. Yes, hit were slow. A man yearned what bread he got that-a-way." Uncle Abner nodded. "And I can recollect my father making gunpowder in one o' them mortars. He'd scrape saltpeter outen the caves—that give the power—and burn red-bud for charcoal—some folks used white walnut—and pound 'em up fine with brimstone. Then he'd moist it and rub it and grain it through a fine sieve. In three or four days he'd make seven or eight pounds o' gunpowder."

Impressed by the slow stream of meal issuing from Uncle Abner's hand mill, the visitor inquires, "Do you have to grind all your meal that way?"

"No, we don't have to. Thar's a leetle tub mill down the creek a mile or tharabouts."

"A tub mill! What's that?"

Uncle Abner looks surprised at such ignorance, but smiles with kind toleration as he proceeds patiently to explain. "When a man lives on a branch or a prong of the creek, whar the water's lasty and thar's a right smart trickle all the time, he puts him in a tub mill, and lets the water grind fer him.

"Ye take a log and hew it till hit's kindly like a tub with a long spindle rising right out'n the midst of it. Run your water in a trough so it'll hit right in the tub and as fast as hit turns o' course the spindle turns too. Then ye fasten your grindin' stone on the top o' your spindle, and thar's your mill. Of course ye make a roof and walls, and put a floor in, and thar's a leetle room for grinding, up above the tub. The spindle goes up through the floor."

"I don't see how people knew how to make all those things."

"They had to. We didn't have no money to buy the tricks and fixin's they had down in the settlements. And we couldn't ha' brung them in hyer, noway. There ain't no roads scarcely yit, and 'twas worse back in them days. A man could fetch jest what he could pack in on his horse— or on his back like as not."

"Why, how did you bring your furniture?"

"Never brung no furniture. Folks made it. My pappy made that bed out'n black warnut."

"But the springs! I know you've got springs on it because I've slept there."

He rises and turns back the feather bed and the corn-shucks mattress beneath. "Jest look at 'em. Hit's a rope bed. They bore them holes in the sides and eends, and thread the rope through 'em and stretch it tight criss-cross. That's all the springs a body needs. Well, I did bring on a leetle table-stand that were kindly purty to pleasure my woman. I carried it on horseback. But commonly we jest bring in some iron and delft, a leetle coffee, some indigo, and alum for dyein'."

"I should think you'd want sugar and soap."

"We allers make our sweetenin' from a sugar-tree, or raise a patch o' sorghum. And everybody makes soap out of ashes. That iron kittle thar's helt many a bilin' o' soap, besides hog-water at butcherin', and clothes every Monday."

"Where do you wash?"

"Thar by the creek, in that battlin' trough. Ye sob 'em and rensh 'em and rub 'em in the trough, and beat 'em with the batler on the battlin' bench."

A poplar log about six feet long had been split in two and turned flat side up. One end had been hollowed out for a washing trough, nearly four feet long and two feet wide. There was a little hole bored in the bottom, with a peg for a drain-plug. The two feet or more at the end that was not hollowed out was smoothed off to battle the clothes upon.

"Well, Uncle Abner, it looks quite like the original washing machine."

"Yes, hit's fer washin'. Battlin's what makes the clothes white—that is, bilin' and battlin'. Course I reckon the soap has a sight to do with it, too. Some women can make soap that jest drives the dirt like a nest o' hornets. Hit's got to git. Yes, sir!"

Uncle Abner emphasizes this efficiency by biting off a fresh chew from a twist of homegrown tobacco. Aunt Sally is sitting on the other side of the hearth placidly smoking.

"Don't you ever smoke, Uncle Abner?"

"No, not scarcely ever. Smokin's all right for a woman that can set around the fire and enjy it, but chawin's a heap convenienter fer a man. Hit don't tie him down nowhar like a pipe."

"Aunt Sally, are all your children married?"

"All but Bradley and Tom. And Tom, he's aimin' to marry him a woman afore long, now."

"Well, you'll be busy about the wedding, won't you?"

"No, young folks don't have no weddin' to speak of, these days. Now, when we war married, there was a heap o' doin's. We had an infare and waiters. I had a waiter, and he had a waiter."

"An infare, Aunt Sally, what's that?"

Aunt Sally sucks several strong puffs of smoke and seems to be lost in retrospection. Uncle Abner takes up the tale.

"Well, an infare weddin' was old-fashioned, one o' them customs the old folks had. Sally's folks gien us a big supper arter the weddin'. Everybody on the creek was thar, that is, the young folks, ye onderstand. I reckon thar must ha' been forty or nigh about. They'd cooked most everything, deer-meat and fried ham and sausage, turkey and chickens, and all sorts of vegetables, and pies and cakes. Arter everybody had eat, they began to frolic and dance. We sat by the fire whilst they ran a set or two, then Sally leaned over and said, 'Ab, why cain't we run a set, too?' I said, 'We can, by ginger.' So we run a set. Then all the fellars wanted to swing Sally, so we danced the Virginia reel. Well, we slept thar that night. Next day we went over to my folks and thar was another supper and another frolic. And the next day arter that we come up hyer, whar I'd built this house. But they don't do that-a-way no more, not commonly, I mean."

No, but that's the way kings and queens used to do. They called their waiter the Lord Chamberlain. It's a custom that must have come down from old, old times.

Almost everything at Uncle Abner's seems to be home-made. His jugs, crocks, and jars are either a rich red or a deep blue, some of them quite shapely. But nearer the stores, indeed, perhaps in most places, the lard pail has driven out home-made pottery. Cedar piggins on the kitchen shelf look like small buckets upside-down. The churn is made in similar fashion. Even the old rifle, lying in the forked sticks nailed against the wall, was made by his uncle, who gained quite a reputation throughout the district as a gunmaker. This, of course, was a mere avocation, pursued at odd times, when other men were sitting around chatting. But his industry did not deprive him of the luxury of gossip, for whenever his little work-shed was open, men gathered there to talk, and the gunsmith could hear all the news and suppositions of the neighborhood without stopping his work.

Every man undertook all ordinary activities for himself. Each was farmer, trapper, builder, carpenter, shoemaker, wagoner, lumberman, raftsman, blacksmith, and stone-mason. Each served as barber, nurse, or undertaker, as occasion required. Every one tanned small pelts, but for the family shoe leather, he went to a tanyard. But a tanyard, saltboiling, and blacksmithing required rather more skill, and soon kept a man busy all the time so that his farming and hunting to procure corn and meat for his family had to be either crowded into his odd moments or done for him by hirelings.

It might be expected that men so adept in all the circumstances of their lives and so resolute and independent in spirit would show capacity for self-government. On surveying their history we find this to be true. Again and again they have shown an inborn skill in self-government, an unusual clear-headedness in organizing and setting up a working constitution, as at Watauga, Mecklenburg, Franklin, and Boonesboro.[1]

Most men of strong individuality and independent mind have the gift of persuasive speech. They can explain their aims and actions clearly, forcibly, and, perhaps most important for the gaining of interest, sympathetically. As might be expected, oratory is a characteristic gift of the Mountain People. Those who do not "foller speakin'" themselves, cordially appreciate oratory in others. Men who cannot read and write are often alert and discriminating judges of thought and speech. Mountain People will travel miles to a "speakin'" and listen for hours with keen and eager enjoyment. They take unusual delight in being swayed by eloquence.

This leads naturally to the consideration of a statement that is inconsistent with the usual conception of the Mountain People and contradic-

[1] See Chapter Three.

tory to much that is written about them. They are frequently referred to as stolid, impassive, listless. As a matter of fact, they have strong and deep feelings, which are both intense and lasting. But their feelings do not play upon the surface of their natures. Their faces are immobile unless deeply stirred. In religion their feelings play a prominent part, leading to extravagant actions in "protracted meetings" and, in the case of the women, at funerals. In the courts of law, where men are not visibly stirred by emotion, they are largely governed by their personal feelings. Evidence has little chance against kinship or enmity. Even in business dealings an opportunity to make money may be declined because of personal feelings.

In sickness, friends and kinsfolk gather, and sometimes seriously impede recovery by crowding into the room and conversing continuously. They are more than willing to sit up all night or do anything else for a sick neighbor; or, in case of an accident, even if not very serious, to make personal sacrifices. The claims of sympathy are paramount. A typical instance will illustrate this: A young cow mired down in thin mud away up on the edge of a steep hill. The mud acted like quicksand, and the helpless animal was sunk to the body before she was discovered. Neighbors gathered, got ropes around her, and dragged her out upon solid ground. She was exhausted and could not stand. Night was falling. It began to snow heavily,—twelve inches fell before morning,—and the cow was wet and chilled. Men went down to the foot of the steep, muddy hill and brought straw and an old carpet on which they laid the animal and covered her. Then they discovered that if she struggled to arise during the night, she would fall off the narrow ledge and be killed. So some of the men cut down young trees for posts, others went down and brought a post hole digger, others a ten-foot gate. With these they struggled up the steep and slippery hillside, holes were dug, posts set, the gate nailed to them, and the cow was protected against falling off the ledge. Some of the men offered to stay up there all night in the snowstorm. The next morning the cow was dragged upon a tarpaulin, and a lot of men all around it eased her down to a place level enough for a one-horse sled. This she was slid upon and dragged away to the barn, where a sling was made for her, her legs and body rubbed to restore circulation, and windproof walls temporarily put up around her. Night was falling the second day when the neighbors left. A day or two earlier these men had been too busy to come and work although they needed the money offered, but because there had been an accident, each man came promptly and would accept absolutely no pay for all his unusual exertion. Such unpaid neighborliness is very common.

In cases of serious sickness any neighbor may be called out of his field, his plowing stopped, and he and his horse requisitioned to go for the doctor. When death occurs, every neighbor is expected to help in taking the news to distant relatives, in making the coffin, digging the grave, or acting as one of the numerous pall-bearers needed to carry the body up to the burial spot.

The Mountain People are not musical as are the Italians or Germans. But one frequently hears the lilt of a song or the recitation of a ballad by the girls and women as they go about their work. At night the twanging of a banjo or the picking of a "dulcimore" comes cheerily out of the darkness as the traveler passes a lonely house. The music of the Mountaineers is, like so many of their possessions, a survival from an earlier day and some of their original airs are cited by so distinguished and authoritative a critic as Cecil J. Sharp as tunes of remarkable beauty. Mr. Sharp has earned our lasting gratitude by snatching these from oblivion and preserving them in permanent form.[1]

The banjo and the dulcimer are used for lyric music: they serve as accompaniment to song. But the chief musical instrument in the Mountains is the violin, which is much used at dances and frolics. This is the reason why many Mountain

---

[1] Campbell and Sharp, *English Folk Songs from the Southern Appalachians.* Putnam.

preachers frown upon it. A visitor from outside is sometimes asked with conscientious wistfulness, "D'ye reckon there's any harm in a fiddle?"

The fiddles, like the banjos and dulcimers, are likely to be homemade, and the tunes have an appealing flavor, a heart-pleasing quality, that seems homemade also. The tunes that have been handed down have been unconsciously modified till they express the movement, scope, and feeling of the individual fiddlers, whose independence is shown even in the way they hold their instruments. One man holds it against his chest instead of under his chin; another stands it upright upon his knee, or lays it along his arm. It is, of course, impossible here to reproduce the music, but its crudeness does not strike the listener as ludicrous, rather, perhaps, as wistful.

Even the names given to it have a quaint homeliness; for example: "Sugar in the Gourd." A dried gourd is a common receptacle for salt or sugar. There is a hearty pleasure in finding that it is not empty. "Billy in the Low Ground," "Walk Along John," "Big Eared Mule," and "Forked Deer" carry their own pleasant associations. "Ways of the World" suggests the strange experiences of a traveler who has been in a town, perhaps into an adjoining county. "Bonaparte's Retreat" and "Napoleon Crossing the Rocky Mountains" suggest even wider travel, mostly by way of the imagination. "Liquor All Gone,"

"Parting Friends," and "Glory in the Meeting House" bring us back to more common experiences, while "Calahan" and "The Last of Sizemore" doubtless originally celebrated men whose deeds though dubious were doughty.

Much has been said of the Mountain man's strength, his skill in hunting and woodcraft, his endurance in the rough pioneer hardships that would seem impossibly formidable to our generation. The Mountain man has, as a rule, less energy of attack than of dogged, unshakable tenacity. He has less dash than a hero of romance, but more endurance. He faces danger, not from a spirit of daring, but because it must be faced. He is courageous, but he inherits the caution of generations of hunters. This caution makes him deliberate. He may not show much eagerness to work in the rain or snow, but he will stand half a day in a drizzling rain to chat with a friend rather than dismiss him with any appearance of discourtesy. He will start over a steep mountain on a dark night of drenching sleet to bring a doctor, to carry out moonshine whiskey, or to go to a dance or a revival meeting. He, and even his wife, will walk thirty or forty miles in a day—a day that begins, perhaps, before dawn and extends into the night.

A woman rises before day, chops some cooking wood, and gets breakfast for the family. Then she milks the cow and eats her own breakfast.

After that she carries a two-year-old baby up into the cove where they are "raisin' the crap." The slope is like the hypotenuse of a triangle, but the child cannot be left at home all day separated from the source of his nourishment. The mother hoes corn all day, and at night drags herself and the baby down to the house again, where she milks the cow, cooks supper, washes up the dishes, and perhaps "washes out a rag or two for the children" before she goes to bed. She works a sixteen-hour day, scarcely gets one baby weaned before the next arrives, and for wages gets a home, the blessings of copious motherhood, and the privilege of wearing her husband's name on her tombstone, which, with all her endurance, is sometimes settled upon her before she is fifty.

Another indication of the vigor of the Mountain People is the size of the family. "Aunt Sally is the mother of eighteen children, and they're all living." "Aunt Betsy Ellen had twenty-two." "Aunt Marthy, up on Hickory Ridge, has twenty-four, fourteen boys and ten gals, and they're every one living, or was the last I knowed." "Aunt Nervie's youngest boy was borned on her fiftieth birthday. She lived to be a hundred and eight years old. Of course he outlived her. He died at ninety-eight. His sister lived to be a hundred and eleven." Similar data can be collected in many neighborhoods.

We should not close this chapter on characteristics without a word upon the manners of the Mountain People. They have not the awkwardness or rawness sometimes found in rural dwellers. There is an unconscious dignity, a quiet courtesy, unspoiled by any conventional forms of politeness. The proprieties are very strictly observed. Children are taught "their manners" with sedulous care. The proprieties and good manners of a primitive and secluded people are, as a matter of course, not the forms prescribed by the diplomatic circles of Washington society. But, judged by inherent dignity and good taste, by sincerity and unhurried serenity, the manners of the Mountain People are probably not inferior to the etiquette generally observed at the White House receptions. I quote an opinion expressed by a keen and trained observer who has had considerable contact with the Mountain People in their own homes:

"They have the finest manners I ever saw, utterly un-self-conscious. They are the only people I ever saw that do not know there are any grades in society. We may try to ignore it, but they do not know it. The Mountain People have kept so many of the basic human qualities that make for culture. They have no thirst for money, so they have leisure to become cultivated. They are real people. We cannot be so real as these contemplative people."

Mountain Speech and Song

Mountain Speech and Song

O YE who in eternal youth
   Speak with a living and creative flood
This universal English, and do stand
Its breathing book; live worthy of that grand
Heroic utterance,—parted, yet a whole,
Far, yet unsevered,—children brave and free
Of the great Mother-tongue, and ye shall be
Lords of an Empire wide as Shakespeare's soul,
Sublime as Milton's immemorial theme,
And rich as Chaucer's speech, and fair as Spenser's dream.

                                  SIDNEY DOBELL
                                       America

CHAPTER FIVE

Mountain Speech and Song

THE language of the Mountain People has been much maligned. It is neither careless nor degraded. Its difference from "United States English" does not indicate a corrupt falling away from modern speech, but rather a survival from the speech of an older day.

There are three aspects of the situation which it were well to distinguish.

(1) In the Mountains our ears are not assailed by slang. The use of slang, the continual iteration of some pet phrase, usually picked up ready-made, to express widely different meanings, tend to impoverish the vocabulary and weaken discrimination in the use of words. From such faults the Mountain People are mostly free.

(2) As the postal service goes everywhere, and books are occasionally found in far-off places, we must not expect to find everybody in the Mountains speaking alike. Even in the remote coves there is often a marked difference between the language of the grandmother and that of the grandchildren who have been "off" for some time at school.

(3) So far as the pioneer circumstances persist, the pioneer language also survives. When new equipment and new activities come in, new words

and new constructions naturally follow. Consequently, in the Mountains one finds language in all states of development. Except where it has suffered from an inundation of outside words, the language has a decided Shakespearean flavor. The Mountain man clings to Shakespearean words, not because he considers them better than modern words, but because he does not know the modern word. He does not need to know the newer vocabulary perhaps because his surroundings and his habits of thought are largely the same as they were in Shakespeare's day. The requirements of life are with him still simple, as befits an outdoor people.

Our magazine writers usually overdo the dialect in stories of Mountain life.[1] They make their characters speak a mongrel jargon. It is true that Mountain speech is a development from Elizabethan English, in which an unusually large number of the old words have survived. Yet even the most remote dweller is not confined solely to Elizabethan phraseology. Indeed, only enough of that phraseology has survived to give his speech a quaint and delightful flavor. It must be heard to be appreciated, yet some observations may be of interest.

Strong preterites are much in use, like *clum* for climbed (Chaucer wrote it *clomb*, and Spenser

[1] Probably no other book pictures so accurately the Mountain People as Louise R. Murdoch's *Almetta of Gabriel's Run*. Published by Meridian Press, New York.

clomben), *drug* for dragged, *wropt* for wrapped (used by the courtly poet Lovelace), *holp* for helped (as in both Chaucer and Shakespeare and the King James Bible). The Mountaineers continue this tradition in *fotch,* as preterite for fetch.

On the other hand, they try to follow the modern trend, making a regular past tense end in *ed.* So they say *throwed, growed, knowed,* and even go out of their way to make a regular form by the addition of *ed* to the other, as "I was borned in April" or "He tosted us the hay." Yet Spenser has a similar doubling of the ending in "loud he yelded."

They say *fur* with Sir Philip Sidney, and *furder* with Lord Bacon (which is, of course, as correct as murder, from murther). They go back to Chaucer and form plurals by adding *es,* especially in words ending in *st;* as post*es,* beast*es,* frost*es,* joist*es* (or jyst*es*), waist*es,* nest*es,* ghost*es,* in which cases the *es* forms a second syllable. With this habit of making plurals, they treat new words with similar thoroughness: "I tell ye, man, trust*es* is wrong." The habit transfers occasionally to verbs, "Hit cost*es* a lot." "The rope twist*es* all up."

When he calls a cow *contrarious,* he has the authority of Milton, and surely in this age of woman's rights he should not be blamed for expanding forefathers into *foreparents. Afeard* is more logical than afraid, and was preferred by

Lady Macbeth. Shakespeare also calls a salad a *sallet*, a bag a *poke*, and an excited state *franzy*. Caliban's *pied ninny*, as also Milton's "meadows trim with daisies pied," come to mind when we hear a boy praise his *pieded* (or *piedy*) cow. Looking through the fence at the frisky calf, he remarks, "Hit's an *antic* calf," without knowing that Hamlet put "an antic disposition on."

The Mountain mother refers to her daughter's skill as "Sally's *sleight* at buttermaking," a use of the word found in Chaucer, and identical with Spenser's "Y-carved with curious sleights." When young folk in love with each other make serious plans, they are said to be *talking*. The same word is used by Regan in *King Lear*.

Begone is in Shakespeare a kingly word spoken to an inferior. In the mountains it is used with a similar contempt, but only in speaking to dogs.

Fletcher writes:

> I will give thee for thy food
> No fish that *useth* in the mud.

and in the mountains we hear "The sheep uses under the clifts," or "The turkeys use in the wheat-patch."

Piers Plowman speaks of a *heap* of people, and Hakluyt uses *allow* for "assume."

Spenser writes *yit* and rimes it with wit. Perhaps no phrase is derided as more uncouth than *mought* for might, yet here again Spenser is our refuge.

> So sound he slept that naught *mought* him awake.

When a mother asks her daughter to "swinge this chicken," she does not know that the same courtly poet wrote:

> The scorching flame sore swinged all his face.

When the father complains that the teacher "spoke mighty short" to the child, he is not intentionally quoting from *As You Like It*.

They still *tole* hogs with corn, and *gorm* their shoes with sticky mud.

The dialect writers pounce with derisive hilarity upon such awkward and slovenly slips as *sech, sence, agin, Scriptur, ventur, natur, yit, yander*. The Queen-mother of Henry VII wrote *seche* for such, and it is evident from the writings of Nash, Beaumont, and other Elizabethans that all these were good usage at that time.

The Mountain man uses *kill up* as Shakespeare does, and also *live up,* and *teach up,* as in teach up the children to have manners. The phrase—"If you give your pigs a good start they'll *grow off*—is similar surely to "off they go." The Mountain mother adds another: "Susie hain't been much to school, but she *learned off*."

Chaucer's friend Gower writes of "a *sighte* of flowers." The phrase still denotes abundance. We still *rive* an oak into shingles, and, like Prince Arthur, use a *handkercher*.

They "git up afore day to git a *soon* start." In *Antony and Cleopatra* Shakespeare writes, "make your soonest haste."

"We rode considerable *peart* and shunned the worst places." Theseus in *A Midsummer Night's Dream* commends the "pert and nimble spirit of youth."

"Whar's the pile of lumber that stood here?" "I've *wasted* it." Which means used or spent, not squandered. Celia in *As You Like It* says, "I like this place and willingly would waste my time in it."

A lad who has never heard of the ocean says, "I live on yan coast." He carries a *budget* on his back, and *spends* his opinions as Othello did. He sees a snake *quiled* up, or warns you that the river is *half-side deep*.

Besides the identified Shakespearean words that have come down like heirlooms, there are in common use many quaint turns of speech that have an old-world dignity and decorum:

"The child fell into the embers."

"I'd love to wash your dishes for a span."

"Yes, I live here, but I don't belong here. I'm just a hireling."

"The children love to prank with the dog."

"Grandsir (Grandsire) owns a big scope o' land."

"Hit's lasty water; stock can drink thar all summer."

"That baby's plumb purty, and hit's as pleasant as the flowers."

"They dug into the Indian grave and found a master pile o' bones."

"The tree's broke down, and gone to nought."

"I've been very throng today." (A Scottish usage.)

The magazine writers charge the Mountain People with being slow and rather stupid, with a very limited vocabulary. Of course the vocabulary of invention and machinery is lacking because mechanical contrivances for sale elsewhere are not commonly found in the Mountains. But the fact is that the Mountain People are, unconsciously of course, unusually skilful with language.

They have one gift that modern speech has largely lost, the ability to make phrases and even words to fit the needs of the occasion; to express the fresh thought or feeling while it is fluttering over their minds. Their speech is still fluid. It is not yet congealed and fossilized into grammar.

They make verbs out of nouns. "The children *prank* with the dog."

Then they go still further, and make an adverb out of the verb. "He did it *unthoughtedly*." "His mill war consid'able damified (damaged)."

We find the exact word with the same meaning in the *Faërie Queene,* and we all still use its negative, indemnify.

"Is the road passable?" "I don't know. Some places the rains has *gouted* it out mightily, and *undermined* it." "Well, you'll have to *surround* them places." Each is vivid, picturesque, and, as it were, measured to order.

"Liza is more *talkier* than Susie."

"Log houses are a heap *endurabler.*"

"He's the workin'est man," "the speakin'est man," "the preachin'est man," "the banjo-pickin'est man," "the weavin'est woman." "We had the hog-killin'est time" does not denote a butchering occasion; but the zest of hunting and killing, the anticipation of eating roast pork and sausage, and the social delight of the excited and happy crowd of noisy neighbors at hog-killing time suggest this epithet for any lively occasion.

"Hits good wheat, but not very *yieldy* on the ground."

"The boys was all *banded* up in the barn." (In *Timon of Athens* "routs of people did about them band.")

"Sheep is *natured* like a deer; they use up high."

"This land is *right natured* for corn."

"Bears air *destructious,* they kill hogs."

"Our folks got *naturalized* to the doctor, and like him."

"I hain't seen my sister in twenty years; I cain't hardly *memorize* her."

"If it don't *disfurnish* ye none, I'll pay ye later."

"Hit'll take a right spell to *moralize* John Will."

"He *rewarded* Bill." This means no gift to Bill, but a reward offered for his apprehension.

"I raised five sons, and none of 'em war ever *warranted*" (arrested on a warrant).

"Cora's strong-minded; she ain't *afeard*."

"We didn't have no *fotch-on* clothes when I was a-raisin'."

As *wealth* is the collective noun made from weal, and *stealth* is the thing one steals, and *spilth* what one spills, so *filth* in the mountains means the weeds or driftwood that fill up, and *blowth* is the mass of blossoms that blow. "There's a good blowth on the fruit trees this year."

The venerable word *buss* (to kiss) has fallen into disrepute in the dictionaries. But it is still uncontaminated in the Mountains. A derivative from it is also found: *bussy*, a sweetheart.

"He *faulted* her" (scolded).

"He's a *main* worker; he has *breskit*." We have a faded relic in "main strength." Brisket we now use only in reference to an animal. We say of a man that he is "chesty," though we do not usually apply this to his physical energy.

We speak of a dress-pattern or a trousers-pattern, meaning not the shape, but the material out of which it is to be made. So we need not be surprised at—"He sawed him a *house-pattern* out of beech."

Their word-making or phrase-making often gives startling vividness. "Do you *foller talkin'?*" Meaning, is that your profession? or do you make a practice of it?

"He's been *a-devillin'* me all morning."

"They married different then, allers had a long graveyard prayer." (At a funeral the preacher doubtless did ample justice to the deceased—and to his own reputation for eloquence.)

"He takes larnin' easy. I reckon he's capacitated to take all the larnin' ye can give him."

"He's a leetle grain *tetchy*" (or tetchous), as was Richard the Third, whose mother said "tetchy and wayward was thy infancy."

"Mammy tried to put the bridle on, but the mare *whipt* her out." We use *beat* with a similar non-physical implication.

"The moon *fulls* tonight."

"She's the *likeliest favored* gal."

"The littl'un's *ashamed* (bashful). She hain't much manners."

"Grannie's been *bedfast* for a long time."

"Do you *want in?*"

"We had a cedar churn, but it fell to *staves*."

"I *aim* to settle down," as frequently in Shakespeare.

"Children grow up *directly*."

"I want to buy a *pretty* for my baby-child. I told her she should have her *happy*."

"He's a mighty *common* man" (affable, mingles with folk as an equal).

When a girl pitched a tune too high, an observer, with a vision in mind of a plow running out of the ground, remarked, "She started it *too shallow*."

"I rode to town for some *iron and delft* (iron pots and pans and dishes).

The language of the Mountain People frequently shows an exactness of thinking that gives an artistic touch to their speech. On the train one inquires, "Is this your paper?" "No, hit belongs to this seat."

Susie, eight years old, on being asked, "Was your new baby a boy?" replies very seriously, "Yes, hit was a boy"; then, after a pause, "and hit's a boy yit."

"Is that a gallon can?" "No, not hardly, I reckon, but hit'll hold quite a content."

This desire for exactness has given such expressions as rifled-gun (often clipped to rifle-gun), rock-clift, ham-meat or ham-bacon, cow-brute, man-person, granny-woman, tooth-dentist, church-house, and biscuit-bread. Bread may mean corn-bread, or simply corn. "I'm clearin' a field to raise my *bread*."

As in language everywhere, there are curious mutations. They take "y" from "yeast," but add it to "earn." "Queer" becomes *quar*, and conversely "care" becomes *keer*. "Chair" becomes *cheer*, "crop" turns to *crap*, and conversely "wrap" becomes *wrop*. An "r" often gets into *warter* (water), *orter* (ought to), *arter* (after), and even invades proper names, as *Cordle* (Caudill) and *Orsborn*.

We need not be surprised at "sarvice-berry" when the *Faërie Queene* has *swarved* for swerved, nor scorn their changing joist to *jiste* and join to *jine,* when the super-elegance of Alexander Pope pronounced them in exactly the same way.

For the pronoun "it," the Chaucerian "hit" is still commonly used. But not always. An indefinable instinct for euphony governs the choice. Probably this same artistic instinct for sound determines the choice between "there" and "thar," "where" and "whar," "is" and "air,",and other locutions defiant of grammar. But the latter phrase is scarcely correct, for of grammar they are entirely unconscious. Here language is still spoken thought, not something written down and analyzed.

There is one exception to this statement. The language of the ballads is handed down, as it were, in carved stone. It is chipped here and there, and occasionally we find puttified restorations, but as a whole the ballads are more or less sacrosanct heirlooms handed down supposedly intact. They are not to be meddled with. Their words remain an outside thing, like a pearl in an oyster. The poetry is not assimilated or absorbed into the personality of the singer. The language, therefore, remains petrified.

Ballads are the poetry of primitive people. They have no individual author, but are the product of communal pride and joy in their common hero, who is often their common ancestor. Ballads could not arise in a cosmopolitan community. It must be homogeneous at least in racial or tribal feeling. There must be a unity of interest. There may be a lord in his castle and his retainers in hovels, but they are all kinsfolk. All are united in a common purpose and a common adventure. Probably all are bound together by a common danger, and all enjoy the common pleasures of the great outdoors. They are, at least, all vitally interested in a common exploit in which all feel that they have a share. One of them has ventured over the border and discomfited the enemy. If not one, perhaps several, but never an army, never an impersonal organization. The ballad is personal. It celebrates personal and individual adventures. Our champion, *my* forty-second cousin, perhaps, dared this deed. One of us, one from our midst, suffered this sorrow, or endured this bitter wrong. The ballad often tells of the exploits of a chief, but the point of view is that of the common people. It gives their rather childish notions of the wealth, luxury, and happiness of their social superiors. These have "milk-white hands," "cherry cheeks," "yellow hair," "ivory combs," "belts of gold." Even their horses are shod with silver and gold. Their refreshment is always the blood-red wine. Their companions or attendants are always three, or seven, or twenty-four.

The old English ballads (it is noteworthy that almost all are in the Scottish form) have been handed down from singer to singer without either book or manuscript. In weathering thus the storms of time, some of the ballads have suffered a sea change. In the "Turkish Lady," for example, Gilbert à Becket (father of the martyred archbishop of Canterbury) had already become "Beichan." This the Mountain singers have further transmuted to "Bateman." They are rather shaky on ethnology, so the Turk is referred to as "The Turkish." "A lord of high degree" is no longer a familiar object, consequently, in the fourth stanza the phrase gets a twist. The second line of the sixth stanza is evidently a mere jingle of words, inserted to fill up the line forgotten by the singer or by one of the singer's ancestors. Not being very familiar with gold, they make, in stanza thirteen, an extravagant valuation of the lady's belt.

Turkish Lady.

1. Lord Bateman was a noble lord, He thought himself of high degree; He could not rest nor be contented Until he had voyaged across the sea.

2. He sailed east and he sailed westward
   Until he reached the Turkish shore;
   And there he was taken and put in prison;
   He lived in hopes of freedom no more.

3. The Turkish had one only daughter,
   The fairest creature eye ever did see.
   She stole the keys to her father's prison,
   Saying, "Lord Bateman I'll set free."

4. "Have you got houses? have you got lands, sir?
   Or do you live at a high degree?
   What will you give to the fair young lady
   That out of prison will set you free?"

5. "I've got houses, and I've got lands, love—
   Half of Northumberland belongs to me,
   And I'll give it all to the Turkish Lady
   If she from prison will set me free."

6. "Seven long years I'll make a vow, sir,
   Seven more by thirty-three,
   And if you'll marry no other lady,
   No other man shall marry me."

7. Then she took him to her father's harbor,
And gave to him a ship of fame;
"Farewell, farewell, to you, Lord Bateman,
I fear I never shall see you again."

8. For seven long years she kept her vow, sir
And seven more by thirty-three.
She gathered all her gay, fine clothing,
Saying, "Lord Bateman I'll go see."

9. She sailed east and she sailed westward,
Until she reached the English shore;
And when she came to Lord Bateman's castle,
She lighted down before the door.

10. "Are these Lord Bateman's gay, fine houses?
And is his lordship here within?"
"Oh yes, oh yes," cried the proud young porter,
"He has just taken his young bride in."

1. "Go tell him to send me a slice of cake,
And draw me a glass of the strongest wine,
And not to forget the fair young lady,
That did release him when close confined."

12. "What news, what news, my proud young porter,
What news, what news have you brought to me?"
"Oh, there is the fairest of all young ladies
That ever my two eyes did see."

13. "She has got rings on every finger,
And on one of them she has got three;
And she's as much gold around her middle
As would buy Northumberland of thee."

14. "She tells you to send her a slice of cake,
And draw her a glass of the strongest wine,
And not forget the fair young lady
That did release you when close confined."

15. Lord Bateman rose from where he was sitting,
    His face did look as white as snow,
    Saying, "If she is the Turkish Lady,
    With her, love, I'm bound to go."

16. Oh, then, he spoke to the young bride's mother,
    "She's none the better nor worse for me;
    She came to me on a horse and saddle,
    And she may go back in a carriage and three."

    "Your daughter came here on a horse and saddle
    And she may return in a chariot free,
    And I'll go marry the Turkish Lady
    That crossed the roaring sea for me."

In the first stanza of "Lord Thomas and Fair Elender," we find the Chaucerian phrase, "rede me a riddle." This has survived because of its euphony, not because of any uncertainty as to his preference on the part of the hero. The older ballad makers always admired yellow or golden hair. "The brown girl," a brunette, though she is rich, is not a favorite, for personal charm, like individual prowess, always ranks high with the pioneer. The second line of the third stanza calls attention to Lord Thomas's "waiters." Completely ignoring the bridegroom, our common usage at weddings alludes to a certain individual as "best man." Mountain usage calls him "waiter." The usual meaning of "wait" in Shakespeare's day was to attend: "We'll wait upon your grace."

Lord Thomas and Fair Elender.

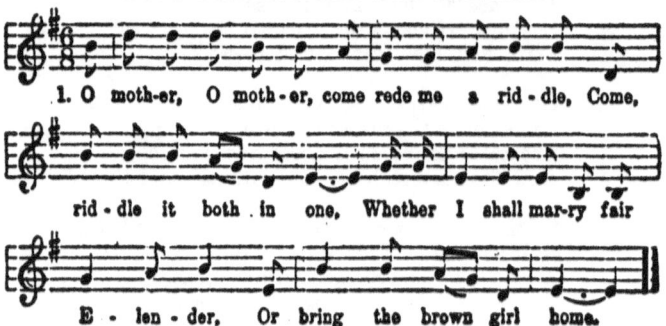

1. O mother, O mother, come rede me a riddle, Come, riddle it both in one, Whether I shall marry fair Elender, Or bring the brown girl home.

2. The brown girl, she has house and lands,
   Fair Elender, she has none;
   Therefore, dear child, under my consent,
   Go bring the brown girl home.

3. He dressed himself in scarlet red;
   His waiters all in green;
   And in every town that he rode through
   They took him to be some king.

4. He rode up to fair Elender's gate;
   He dingled so loud on the ring,[1]
   There's no one so ready as fair Elender
   To rise and welcome him in.

5. What news, what news, Lord Thomas? she said,
   What news have you brought unto me?
   I come to ask you to my wedding,
   The brown girl the bride to be.

6. Mother, O Mother, come rede me a riddle,
   Come riddle it both in one,
   Whether to go to Lord Thomas' wedding
   Or tarry this day at home.

[1] Before doorbells were invented, a visitor could make considerable noise at the front door, dingling the large ring in its socket.

7. Many a one may be your friend,
   And many a one your foe;
   If I should advise you to do best,
   It's tarry this day at home.

8. Many a one may be my friend,
   And many a one my foe;
   I'll venture, I'll venture my own heart's blood
   To Lord Thomas' wedding I'll go.

9. She dressed herself in satin so white,
   And her waiting maids in green,
   And in every town that she rode through
   They took her to be some queen.

10. She rode up to Lord Thomas' gate,
    She dingled so loud on the ring,
    There's no one so ready as Lord Thomas himself
    To rise and welcome her in.

11. He took her by the lily-white hand,
    He led her through the hall,
    And seated her at the table's head
    Amongst the nobles all.

12. Is this your bride, Lord Thomas, she said,
    That looks so wonderful brown,
    When you might have married as fair a lady
    As ever the sun shined on.

13. Dispraise her not, fair Ellen, he said,
    Dispraise her not unto me,
    For I think more of your little finger
    Than I do of her whole body.

14. The brown girl had a little pen-knife;[1]
    It was both keen and sharp;
    Between the short ribs and the long
    She pierced fair Elender's heart.

[1] A small sharp knife used to cut a goose quill for writing.

15. What's the matter, fair Ellen? he said.
   You look so pale and wan;
   You once did bear as good a color
   As ever the sun shined on.

16. Oh, are you blind, Lord Thomas? she said,
   Or can't you so very well see?
   Don't you see my own heart's blood
   Come trinkling down my knee?

17. He took the brown girl by the hand
   And led her over the hall,
   And with his sword he cut off her head
   And pitched it against the wall.

18. He put the handle against the wall,
   The point against his breast,
   Adieu, adieu to three dear loves,
   God send them all to rest.

19. Go dig my grave both long and large,
   And dig it wide and deep,
   And bury fair Elender in my arms,
   The brown girl at my feet.

Perhaps the most famous of all the ballads is "Barbara Allen." It has sung itself with plaintive sweetness into the hearts of many generations. In this ballad we note that the English "month of May" retains its alliterative hold, though the Mountain season is much earlier. The death-bell also remains intact, because of its melancholy appeal, though of course this Catholic custom has never been practiced in the Mountains. The "west countree," however, is changed to the western states.

Barbara Allen.

1. In Scarlet Town, where I was born, There was a fair maid dwelling, Made

ev-'ry youth cry, "Well-a-day," Her name was Bar-bara Al-len.

2. All in the merry month of May,
   When the green buds they were swelling,
   Sweet William came from the western states
   And courted Barbara Allen.

3. It was all in the month of June
   When all things they were blooming,
   Sweet William on his death-bed lay,
   For the love of Barbara Allen.

4. He sent his servant to the town,
   Where Barbara was a-dwelling,
   My master is sick and sent for you
   If your name is Barbara Allen.

5. And death is painted on his face,
   And o'er his heart is stealing,
   Then hasten away to comfort him,
   O lovely Barbara Allen.

6. So, slowly, slowly, she got up,
   And slowly she came nigh him;
   And all she said when she got there,
   Young man, I think you are dying.

7. Oh, yes, I'm sick, and very sick,
   For death is on me dwelling;
   No better, no better I never can be,
   If I can't get Barbara Allen.

8. Oh, yes, you are sick, and very sick,
   And death is on you dwelling,
   No better, no better you never will be,
   For you can't get Barbara Allen.

9. Oh, don't you remember in yonder town
   When you were at the tavern
   You drank a health to the ladies all 'round,
   And slighted Barbara Allen?

10. Oh, yes, I remember in yonder town,
    In yonder town a-drinking,
    I gave a health to the ladies all 'round,
    But my heart to Barbara Allen.

11. He turned his pale face to the wall,
    And death was with him dealing,
    Adieu, adieu to my friends all around,
    Be kind to Barbara Allen.

12. As she was on her highway home,
    The birds they kept a-singing,
    They sang so clear they seemed to say,
    "Hard-hearted Barbara Allen."

13. As she was walking o'er the fields,
    She heard the death bell knelling,
    And every stroke did seem to say
    "Hard-hearted Barbara Allen."

14. She looked to the east and she looked to the west,
    She spied his corpse a-coming.
    Lay down, lay down, the corpse of clay,
    That I may look upon him.

15. The more she looked, the more she mourned,
    Till she fell to the ground a-crying,
    Saying, Take me up and carry me home,
    For I am now a-dying.

16. O Mother, O Mother, go make my bed,
    Go make it long and narrow;
    Sweet William died for pure, pure love,
    And I shall die for sorrow.

17. O Father, O Father, go dig my grave,
    Go dig it long and narrow;
    Sweet Wiliam died for me today,
    I'll die for him tomorrow.

18. She was buried in the old church yard,
    And he was buried a-nigh her.
    On William's grave there grew a red rose,
    And on Barbara's grew a green brier.

19. They grew to the top of the old church wall,
    Till they couldn't grow any higher;
    They lapped and they tied in a true lover's knot,
    And the rose grew around the brier.

Many of the ballads have a refrain in which all the auditors may join. Sometimes the refrain has no connection with the story, as in the short lines of "The Two Sisters." "Bowee down!" and "Bow and balance to me!" are a remnant from an old dance jingle, which was occasionally sung by dancers even after the music was furnished by the fiddle. "Bowee" was originally "Bow ye," but it has dropped the "y" and become "bowee," as is common in Scottish familiar speech. The triple repetition of the first line in every stanza is a frequent characteristic of ballads,—it gives intensity to the tale.

The Two Sisters.
(The Mill-dam of Binnorie.)

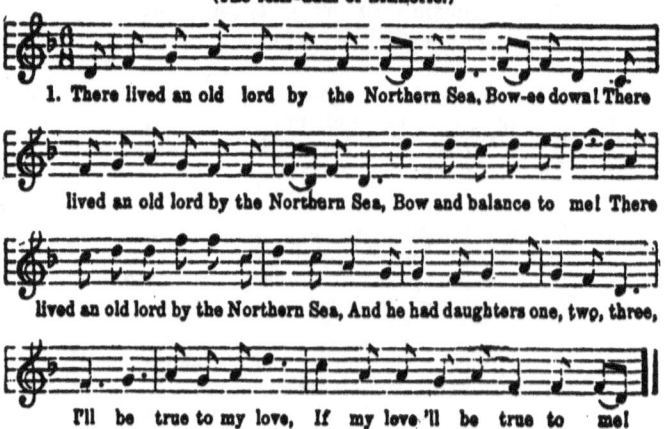

1. There lived an old lord by the Northern Sea, Bow-ee down! There lived an old lord by the Northern Sea, Bow and balance to me! There lived an old lord by the Northern Sea, And he had daughters one, two, three, I'll be true to my love, If my love'll be true to me!

2. A young man came a-courting there,
   Bowee down!
   A young man came a-courting there,
   Bow and balance to me!
   A young man came a-courting there,
   And he made choice of the youngest fair.
   I'll be true to my love,
   If my love'll be true to me!

3. He brought this youngest a beaver hat,
   And the oldest sister didn't like that.

4. As they walked down to the water's brim,
   The oldest pushed the youngest in.

5. O sister, O sister, lend me your hand
   And you may have my house and land.

6. She floated down to the miller's dam,
   The miller drew her safe to land.

Mountain Speech and Song 119

7. And off of her fingers took five gold rings,
   Then into the water he plunged her again.

8. The miller was hanged on a gallows so high,
   The oldest sister there close by.

Ballads, being the literature of the uncultured, naturally seize upon domestic tragedies more often than upon joys,—do we not see the same avidity today in the newspapers?—and gypsies like those in *The Gypsy Laddie* have always been fascinating, partly because of their mysterious coming and going.

The broken rimes of the seventh stanza indicate that the singer (or some singer among her ancestors) forgot the lines, and perhaps condensed two stanzas into one.

2. It's he caught up his old grey horse,
   And he caught up his pony;
   He rode all night and he rode all day
   Till he overtook his doney.[1]

3. It's come go back, my dearest dear,
   It's come go back, my honey,
   It's come go back, my dearest dear,
   And you never shall lack for money.

4. I won't go back, my dearest dear,
   Nor I won't go back, my honey;
   I wouldn't give a kiss from my gypsy's lips
   For you and all your money.

5. It's go pull off those snow-white gloves
   A-made of Spanish leather,
   And give to me your lily-white hand
   And bid me farewell forever.

6. It's she pulled off those snow-white gloves
   A-made of Spanish leather,
   And gave to him her lily-white hand
   And bade him farewell forever.

7. I once did have so many fine things,
   Fine feather-beds and money;
   But now my bed is made of hay
   And the gypsies a-dancing around me.

The ballad of "The Green Willow Tree" does not go back beyond the time of Queen Elizabeth. An English variant gives the Captain as Sir Walter Raleigh, and his ship's name "The Golden Vanity." Doubtless Vanitee became Vanitree, then the first part of the word was variously changed to "make sense" to "The Mary Golden

[1] Doney is a Mountain word for sweetheart, doubtless from the Spanish *donna*.

Tree" (Merry), "The Green Willow Tree," and "The Weeping Willow Tree." In one variant the "Golden" has been transferred to the Turkish ship, "The Golden Silveree." In one version the Sailor Boy refrains from boring holes in the false Captain's ship for the sake of the crew; in another, for the sake of the Captain's daughter— who is supposedly on board; and in a third, for both "your daughter and your men."

The Green Willow Tree.

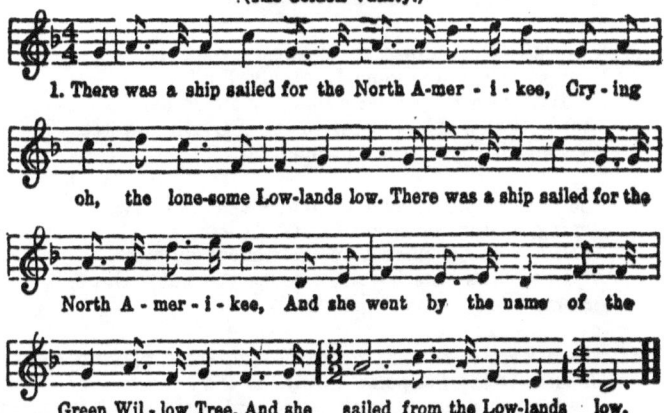

2. She'd only been a-sailing for two weeks or three—
Crying, O the lonesome Lowlands low—[1]
She'd only been a-sailing for two weeks or three,
Till she was overtaken by the Turkish Reveree [2]
As she sailed from the Lowlands low.

[1] Lowlands usually referred to Holland.
[2] Doubtless a form of the Scottish word for robber, *reiver*.

3. Then said the captain, What shall we do?
   Crying, O the lonesome Lowlands low!
   Then said the captain, What shall we do?
   The Turkish Reveree will surely cut us in two!
   As we sail from the Lowlands low.

4. Up spake a sailor boy, What will you give to me,
   Crying, O the lonesome Lowlands low!
   Up spake a sailor boy, What will you give me,
   If I will go and sink for you the Turkish Reveree
   As we sail from the Lowlands low?

5. I'll give you gold, I'll give you fee,
   Crying, O the lonesome Lowlands low!
   I'll give you gold, I'll give you fee,
   And my only daughter for your wedded wife to be!
   As we sailed from the Lowlands low.

6. The lad leapt down and away swam he,
   Crying, O the lonesome Lowlands low!
   He fell upon his breast and away swam he,
   And he swam till he came to the Turkish Reveree,
   As we sailed from the Lowlands low.

7. Then out of his pocket an instrument he drew,
   Crying, O the lonesome Lowlands low!
   Then out of his pocket an instrument he drew,
   And he bored nine holes for to let the water through,
   As we sailed from the Lowlands low.

8. There were some playing cards and some playing checks,
   Crying, O the lonesome Lowlands low!
   There were some playing cards and some playing checks,
   And before they cleared the boards, they were in water to
       their necks!
   As we sailed from the Lowlands low.

9. Then the lad turned back and away swam he,
   Crying, O the lonesome Lowlands low!
   Then he fell upon his breast and away swam he,
   And he swam till he came to the Green Willow Tree,
   As we sailed from the Lowlands low.

10. Cried he, Kind Captain, I have done your decree,
    Crying, O the lonesome Lowlands low!
    Cried he, Kind Captain, I have done your decree,
    Now take me on board ere I perish in the sea!
    As we sailed from the Lowlands low.

11. Nay, nay, sailor boy, I'll never take you on board,
    Crying, O the lonesome Lowlands low!
    Nay, nay, sailor boy, I'll never take you on board;
    Never will I be to you as good as my word!
    As we sailed from the Lowlands low.

12. 'Tis only the respect that I have for your crew,
    Crying, O the lonesome Lowlands low!
    'Tis only the respect that I have for your crew
    Or I'd sink your ship and you with it too!
    As we sailed from the Lowlands low.

13. Then he fell upon his breast and away swam he,
    Crying, O the lonesome Lowlands low!
    He fell upon his breast and away swam he;
    Adieu, adieu to the Green Willow Tree!
    Adieu to the Lowlands low.

Either the passage of time or change in environment sometimes led to an interesting change in a ballad as sung in the Mountains. For example, in "The Demon Lover," which space does not permit us to include, the ship carpenter becomes the house-carpenter, a more familiar occupation. The lover's cloven hoofs are omitted and nothing remains in the ballad to show that he is a demon. This is also a good example of the "answering ballad," which probably grew out of the "flyting" (Scottish for scolding) ballad, in which two persons conduct a sort of debate and "answer back."

"Come, all ye Fair and Tender Ladies," is

124 *The Land of Saddle-bags*

more of a song than a ballad. In the first stanza the word "court" is used, not in the sense of actively wooing, but it indicates a gracious and courtly reception of their attentions.

Come, all ye Fair and Tender Ladies.

1. Come, all ye fair and ten-der la-dies. Take warning how you court young men. They're like a star in the sum-mer morn-ing. They'll first ap-pear and then they're gone.

2. They'll tell to you some loving story
   And make you think that they love you true;
   Straightway they'll go and court some other,
   Oh, that is the love they have for you.

3. If I had known before I courted,
   That love had been so hard to gain
   I'd have locked my heart in a box of golden,
   And fastened it up with a silver chain.

4. I wish I were some little sparrow,
   And I had wings and I could fly,
   I'd fly away to my false true-love,
   And when he'd talk I would be by.

5. But as it is I am no sparrow,
   I have no wings, nor can I fly,
   I sit down here in a grief and sorrow
   And try to pass my troubles by.

Moonshine and Feuds

Moonshine and Feuds

THE North of Ireland was settled by Scotchmen who had been imported by James I.—They learned how to make poteen in little stills after the Irish fashion. By-and-by these Scotch-Irish fell out with the British government, and large bodies of them emigrated to America.—They were a fighting race.—They brought with them, too, an undying hatred of excise laws, and a spirit of unhesitative resistance to any authority that sought to enforce such laws.

KEPHART
Our Southern Highlanders

CHAPTER SIX

Moonshine and Feuds

"WHY do those Mountaineers make moonshine?" Well, why did your great-great-grandparents make it? They turned their barley and corn into whiskey, their fruit into brandy, and their blackberries into cordial. That was as regular a part of a thrifty housewife's program as the canning of fruit and vegetables is today. Somewhere along the line between these highly respected ancestors and yourself the practice of making New England rum or Virginia brandy was discontinued as not quite suitable for a deacon or a vestryman. Gradually these other products fell into disfavor also, until within a generation or so even the old cider barrel has given place to canned cider. Perhaps you remember that your dear old Grandmother insisted as long as she lived that *home-made* blackberry cordial never did a mite of harm to anybody.

The most obvious answer to any question about Mountain usage is, it is a survival from the older day. It has come down among us comparatively unchanged, while on your side of the Mountains the old custom has been worn away in the conflicting currents of modern life.

But there is another answer to the query why

the Mountain People so universally make moonshine. It is a startling answer. *They do not.* Very few Mountain men make moonshine. Perhaps as great a proportion of Mountain men are engaged in distilling illicit whiskey as the proportion of St. Louis or New York men who are engaged in burglary. It is unfair in each case to bring the charge against the entire population. Many counties in the Mountains were dry before their state voted against whiskey. Mitchell County voted dry long before the more "civilized" parts of North Carolina.

We might go further. Even in the case of those who do run a moonshine still the comparison is unjust. Making one's own moonshine may be a crime against the far-off government at Washington, but by Hector! it is not an offence against your neighbor's property or his life. The moonshiner probably pays his debts, is honest in his business dealings, and is a sympathetic and helpful neighbor, "a mighty 'commo*dat*in' man." No one can say that of the burglar.

In the Mountains the morality of any course of action is still judged individualistically. Such considerations do not include its general influence upon the community. This explains why it is that the majority of a community, while disapproving the moonshiner's action, look upon it merely as a matter of personal conduct—like dancing, or playing the fiddle. Such things are not seemly in church members, but they are none of our business. There is, of course, in many instances considerable fear of angering these bold men that defy the law. But back of this fear is the common feeling that it is not our business; and a man that interferes in another man's business deserves whatever he gets. Minding one's own business is a fundamental virtue of the Mountain People.

Let us ask a disapproving citizen how many moonshine stills there are in his community. "Oh, there ain't scarcely none in this deestrict."

"Of course. But how many are there between Bad Creek and Wolf Mountain?"

He begins to count. "Well, there's one, two, three, four—there's about seventeen, I reckon. Of course I don't know, pint-blank, ary one; but I reckon, without an acci*dent*, a body could find 'em." If you are neither a revenue officer nor "one o' them writin' fellers that jest puorely lies about us folks for money," it is not improbable that you may get a moonshiner to express his opinion. Mr. Horace Kephart, having established his honesty in both these particulars, gives us a fair specimen:

"You think the Government tax on whiskey is an imposition. . . . Hit is. . . . Revenue costs a dollar and ten cents on twenty cents' worth o' liquor; and that's robbing the people with a gun to their faces. . . . Whiskey means more to us mountain folk than hit does to folks in town, whar thar's drug-stores and doctors. Let ary thing go wrong in the family—fever, or snake-bite, or somethin'—and we can't git a doctor up hyar less'n three days; and it costs scand'lous. The only medicines we-uns has is yerbs, which customarily ain't no good 'thout a leetle grain o' whiskey. . . . Now, yan's my field o' corn. I gather the corn and shuck hit and grind hit my own self, and the woman she bakes us a pone o' bread to eat —and I don't pay no tax, do I? Then why can't I make some o' my corn into pure whiskey to drink, without payin' tax? I tell you, *'tain't fair,* this way the Government does! But, when all's said and done, the main reason for this 'moonshining,' as you-uns calls it, is bad roads."

"Bad roads!" I exclaimed. "What the—"

"Jest thisaway: From hyar to the railroad is seventeen miles, with two mountains to cross; and you've seed that road. Seven hundred pounds is all the load a good team can haul over that road when the weather's good. . . . Hit takes three days to make the round trip, less'n you break an axle, and then hit takes four. . . . The only farm produce we-uns can sell is corn. You see for yourself that corn can't be shipped outen hyar. . . . Corn *juice* is about all we can tote around over the country and git cash money for. Why, man, that's the only way some folks has o' payin' their taxes!"

"But aside from the work and worry," I remarked, "there is the danger of being shot in this business!"

"Oh, we-uns don't lay *that* up agin the Government. Hit's as fair for one as 'tis for t'other. When a revenuer comes sneakin' around, why, whut he gits, or whut we-uns gits, that's a 'fortune of war,' as the old sayin' is."'

---

[1] Horace Kephart: *Our Southern Highlanders,* Outing Publishing Company, 1913, p. 121. This is the most interesting book on the subject, and for the ground it covers, the most detailed and accurate.

The operation of distilling whiskey has in recent years become as well known in the most favored districts as in the Mountains. The process in the Mountains, if not simpler, is at least managed with simpler and cruder apparatus. A retort is often made from a large iron kettle, used outdoors on wash days and in soap-making and hog-scalding seasons. A small inverted barrel is fitted snugly into this kettle. A pipe is inserted into an augur hole in the bottom (now the top) of the still, and this pipe is bent into a spiral to convey the vapors through a barrel of cold running water.

Corn is moistened and kept warm till it sprouts. It is then dried and carried, usually by night, to a little tub mill to be ground secretly, for grinding such corn is a federal offense. From this "sweet meal" a mash is made with hot water. To this some yeasty material is added and fermentation begins. For more than a week it must be kept just warm enough to ferment. (In the poor shelters many a batch "chills down" and is lost.) After it ferments, this "beer" is poured into the still, the fire lighted, and the vapors start through the copper spiral pipe. Cooled by the running water surrounding the "worm," the vapors condense into a liquid called "singlings" which drips or runs into a receptacle. After the "run" is finished, the still is emptied and the singlings poured in it to be distilled a second time into "doublings," which are thus freed from the rank oils and other impurities. While still warm, the whiskey is put into jugs and carried away for immediate sale.

The making of moonshine is sleepless, nerve-racking work, and produces comparatively little return for the long days and nights of strain. It is a last resource to get money in order to pay taxes, or a persistent doctor, or a yet more importunate lawyer. "Hit's a mighty oneasy way for a man to yearn him some cash money, but looks like we hain't much choice up in this rough country." This latter adjective is applied to the geography, not to the people. There is no shame, no sense of guilt in making or selling this "blockade" whiskey. For prudential reasons, of course, the still and the liquor must be kept concealed. There are always men in the neighborhood that might give information to the sheriff, not usually for a reward, but to satisfy some grievance or grudge against the "blockader." This term, by the way, is fully as common as "moonshine" and "moonshiner." The caution, the excitement, the danger of running a boat through an enemy's blockade, is similar enough to the experiences incurred in illicit distilling to make the term "blockading" entirely suitable.

The liquor is sometimes offered for sale in the vicinity, but in many cases it is carried over the mountain at night on paths too steep for most of us in daylight. Occasionally the thirsty neighbors are invited to buy. The method of advertising is probably not included among the activities of the most approved publicity agencies. If you happened to be wandering on the mountain side where it was "rough," you might—or you might not—notice a twig or bush that had apparently been thoughtlessly cut by somebody trying the edge of his knife, and then thrown down in the path. But the enlightened one would follow the direction of its stem, and in due time find a succession of bushes, each pointing the thirsty traveler onwards to the desired haven. This reminds us of the saying current in Shakespeare's day: "Good wine needs no bush." But the bush that advertised the wine was probably not used in the same fashion.

Not only is it important that the still be hidden, it must also be located near a good spring, which can furnish cold water to cool the copper worm. This necessity for cold water rules out many places that would be entirely safe from observation or access. The smoke, the smell, and even the taste of the water in the brook, would publish undesirable facts, so the still must be located as far from habitation and travel as possible. Away up under a "clift" a spring must be selected that flows under an impenetrable thicket of laurel (rhododendron), or among locust and blackberry briers, in a spot where no wood cutters will be going about, nor any man looking for his stray hogs.

The habit of tippling or dramming is not uncommon. But the men that drink heavily do so only on great occasions which they "celebrate" by drinking steadily until completely intoxicated. They celebrate on Christmas, election day, or any other day that strikes them as worthy of such exuberant attention. But such conduct meets the disapproval of good citizens. "I call sich as that mighty sorry doin's." "Hit's no-caount fellers that follers drinkin' and drammin'." "They drink awhile an then they gits to quarr'lin' an shootin'. Seems like we Mountain folks hain't got good sense." This confession is remarkable in two respects. The man making it has excellent sense and sound judgment. It is also noteworthy for the consciousness of solidarity it reveals— "we Mountain folks." In most places such a commentator would express the gulf that he feels to be between himself and such unworthy people. He would make clear the difference between himself and them. But the sense of loyalty to kith and kin is so strong in the Mountains that the good man often expresses himself as sharing the guilt and folly of those that have no kinship nor claim upon him, except that he and they are all Mountain men.

I once asked a County Judge about the attitude women take towards liquor. He said, "Well, more'n likely they wouldn't drink with you, but if I were to take a bottle along, I reckon most of the women between here and Coal Creek would take a drink with me.'' Possibly a majority of the women *of his own age* in that district might take a drink, but the Judge's estimate was mere guess work, for he himself was known to be ''mighty pizen agin whiskey.'' Whenever I have led up to the subject, the opinion of the women voluntarily expressed has been either regret or indignation at the ravages of whiskey. With a mild, scarcely protesting pathos, a mother remarks, ''Three of my boys has been shot to death; all, ye might say, by whiskey.'' Another, with an edge to her tone, says, ''Them men that makes whiskey, and sells it to our boys—I wish I was on the jury, I'd penetentiar' 'em every time.'' Then with a gleam of fire in her eyes she drops her voice, '' I wouldn't keer if they was in the graveyard.'' Or perhaps, with a rather unhopeful touch of fatalism, ''I wish to the Lord we could get shet of the whiskey.''

It might naturally be expected, in a country where so many men carry weapons, that heavy drinking would result in numerous ''frays.'' This is the case, and these frays generally prove fatal. But even in the roughest sections, public opinion is setting more and more strongly against such outrage against the community. ''Hit used to be,'' said a Judge, ''that when a man killed another, all his friends rushed in and went on his bail. But now the sympathy's all with the corpse.''

In writing of feuds and of the conditions of the country in which feuds exist, Horace Kephart says:[1]

In my own county, and all those adjoining it, there has been only one case of highway robbery, and only one of murder for money, so far as I can learn, in the past forty years.

The most hideous feature of the feud is the shooting down of unarmed or unwarned men. Assassination, in our modern eyes, is the last and lowest infamy of a coward. Such it truly is when committed in the civilized society of our day. But in studying primitive races, or in going back along the line of our own ancestry to the civilized society of two centuries ago, we must face and acknowledge the strange paradox of a valorous and honorable people (according to their lights) who, in certain cases, practiced assassination without compunction and, in fact, with pride.

It is very difficult for an outsider to understand the situation or to sense the atmosphere in which a feud becomes possible, indeed almost inevitable. In the early pioneer days life was a struggle for existence. Men strove not only with the soil and the wilderness, but also with wild beasts, hostile Indians, and, occasionally, with lawless white men. Indians usually fought from ambush. They concealed themselves behind trees and rocks. They crept up stealthily and took their enemy by surprise. The pioneers soon learned to fight the Indians by their own method. This hunter's instinct of stealthily stalking one's prey still persists, whether they be hunting deer, bear, or men.

[1] *Our Southern Highlanders,* pp. 193, 348.

In those old days courts were far away, near the Atlantic coast. There was no police power, no sheriff, no constable, within five hundred miles. Imagine yourself and a few friends marooned upon Robinson Crusoe's island. If a boatful of pirates should land, drunk, insolent, and threatening, what would you do? In such circumstances it is do or die, with no time for hesitation. Our foreparents had to deal with rough and truculent disturbers as best they could. In the absence of law courts, sheriffs, and constables, every man was compelled to take matters into his own hand. Under such conditions good men were patient, cautious, and reserved, but they were courageous, prompt, and thorough. They fought their own fights, and they fought to a finish. A half-beaten enemy is likely to seek a terrible and treacherous revenge, therefore the pioneer, in self-defence, punished thoroughly, usually by death.

To us, protected by adequate police power and a strong public opinion, and far removed from the single-handed pioneer's constant perils, his fighting seems needlessly savage, inhumanly brutal and cruel. But to the pioneer it was simply necessary. "He had it to do." This modern phrase indicates an attitude of mind in which the pioneer habit of suspicious and thorough self-defence too often persists even now.

Before the pioneer conditions and state of mind had wholly disappeared, there came the Civil War.

It aroused men's passions, not against a foreign foe, but against neighbors and kinsmen. While the great majority of the Mountain People, like Lincoln himself, were on the side of the Union, there was all around the borders of the Mountain region a division of sentiment. One neighbor enlisted in the Union Army, another with the Confederates. In these border areas there was naturally a lot of pillaging, counter pillaging, and organizing of Home Guards, seldom officially recognized. All this resulted in a sort of irregular guerrilla warfare, which differed from private murder only in having the resentful approval of a large part of the community. That is to say, the virus of murder was injected into the whole community, so that the people became a sort of absentee mob, if not consenting to these murders, at least condoning them.

Tom ———— lived on a projecting splinter of the Mountains that was almost surrounded with Confederate sympathizers. Tom got word that a gang of these neighbors was coming to compel him to enlist in the Confederate army or to kill him. So he "hid out" for a few days until he could get a chance to get away and join the Union army.

The neighbors came and tried to make Tom's wife tell where he was hidden. As she refused, they took her out to the rail fence in the yard, lifted the panel of rails, spread out her hands upon the lower rail, replaced the heavy rails upon her fingers, and some of the men added to the agony by climbing upon the fence, to add more weight to the crushing of her fingers. She still refused to betray her husband's hiding-place.

When, after the war, Tom returned, is it any wonder that he got from his wife the names of her tormentors and, lying in wait for them, one by one, finally killed seven of them? The general comment of the mountain neighbors was, "Tom'll git 'em all afore he's done. And killin's too good fer 'em."

This unrepudiating attitude of mind, this acceptance of murder as a natural social policy, strongly tinged the community consciousness in these places, and it has taken a long time to fade out.

It is a significant fact that most of the feudists were boys during the awful days of the Civil War. Their minds were saturated with bloodshed, and they were cursed with the greatest evil of civil war, the poison of individual and personal hatred, not against unreal or remote creatures of romance, but against neighbors. Nothing pertaining to war is more devilish than the development of that state of mind in which one believes all evil that is spoken or insinuated about his neighbors. This is the atmosphere of the feud.

Any sort of dispute in any city may start a fight in which men are killed. But a fight is not a feud. There can be no feud without a social fabric of interwoven kinship. A feud grows out of exaggerated loyalty to one's family, when the family has lived in one community so long, has intermarried so persistently, and has been shut away from all impact of outsiders so completely that half the folk in the county are "blood kin."

But if they are all kin, whom would they fight against? They fight against each other. The kinsmen are not all on one side. No one can tell beforehand who will line up on either side. There are always unexpected turns as the "war" goes on, and unexpected people are drawn into it. It is true the spark, like a slow match, runs along the lines of kinship. It is a man's kinship, or the public knowledge of it, that makes it almost impossible for him to avoid suspicion and attack from one side or the other. But nobody can foretell where the flame will burst out or from which side the attack will come. Casual writers do not observe all the facts; consequently, they cannot understand the situation, and unintentionally they give a distorted impression.

Even with this background of consanguinity, together with the pioneer instinct of personal self-defence and the bloody-minded inheritance of war, a murderous quarrel does not develop into a feud until it gets into politics. I do not mean that they always quarreled about politics. The original cause of contention might be a business contract, the ownership of some half-wild hogs, the treatment of a woman, or any of the thousand other things that men fight about. But if the courts of justice could remain impartial and masterful, the fighting would be checked before it could become a feud. Each party knows that the other will seek to elect its own partisans to the offices that control or influence the machinery of the law. It is very important that we have the judge, the sheriff, the marshal, the jailer, on our side. If our enemies get possession of these offices, it is equivalent to the death of the accused man either by skilful manipulation of the legal machinery or, failing that, by secret assassination when he is unarmed and helpless. In these circumstances, the election of this man or that as sheriff means life or death to a good many people. Political strife in most places is for money or ambition; here it meant life or death.

A word ought to be said in defence of the courts of law. In a neighborhood where the population has intermarried for generations, until everybody is the cousin of everybody else, it is difficult to get a jury to convict. Witnesses do not care to incur the enmity of the accused or of his kinsfolk. The sheriff connives at the escape of his cousin. Someone on the jury is sure to be a far-off kinsman. So even if the judge is untrammeled by consanguinity, he is often helpless. Occasionally the officers are not merely inefficient, but they are positively and partisanly corrupt. They bring false charges, they arrest the innocent victim, disarm him, and stand by while their kinsmen murder him.

Under such conditions when two men quarrel, the kinsfolk on both sides, especially the immediate families, are expecting attack and get their guns and ammunition ready. This suspicious attitude, this nervous tension, together with the jolting of their calmer judgment by bitter talk and whiskey, adds the spark to the individual "preparedness," and it flames up into a feud.

Revenge is not, as is sometimes stated, the main cause of a feud, but rather suspicion and the instinct for self-defence, coupled with wide-spread distrust of the courts and officers of law. Suppose a man kills your father and is not arrested because the sheriff is his cousin. You make no attempt to kill him. But when he thinks it over, talks it over with hot-headed kinsmen, and drinks it over in white whiskey, he concludes that you will be sure to waylay him, therefore he had better kill you also to be safe. He does. Gathered around your coffin, your family and kinsfolk reason that his next move will be to kill your brother, so they decide to "get" him before he shoots any more of the family—very natural reasoning under the circumstances. Why are the advocates of national preparedness so shocked at this individual preparedness?

A feud almost always arises from the arrogance and half-drunken bullying of armed men. Such fellows, idle, drinking, quarrelsome, band together, perhaps for minor depredations. Men avoid them as much as possible and endure a good deal of annoyance till some man, driven beyond all patience, resists, and there is a fight in which one is killed, perhaps both. Usually, on account of the numbers, it is the innocent man that is killed, and the murderers grow still more insolent and defiant. Then if, for reasons of kinship or cowardice, the sheriff, or judge, or jury do nothing, the slain man's relatives naturally arm themselves, either for revenge or, more likely, for self-protection.

A feud never arises except from the impotence of justice and that impotence often arises from the shrewd manipulation of the machinery of the law in the interest of the law breaker. When the law that should protect the peaceable citizens and punish the outrageous becomes by juggled elections a strong weapon in the hands of the lawless, and there is no hope of wresting it from them, then the victims resort to bloody resistance and armed force. Whiskey complicates the situation, arouses devilish passions, and, by removing the inhibitions of prudence and fairmindedness, incites men to instant and fierce aggression. In some feuds one side is honorable and law-abiding; its members are driven to take up arms in self-defence. Its leaders practice great self-restraint and hold their followers back from the reckless blood-lust and murderous practices of their opponents. But even so, some of their less high-minded followers occasionally break over in a fit of exasperation and slay opponents with their enemies' own savagery. This is an inevitable result of war, either public or private. Whether waged by a nation or by a family, it is wholly demoralizing. Public and private war alike grow out of the blindness and selfish greed of society, which makes no adequate constructive preparations for peace, but heedlessly permits inflammable material to accumulate until explosion and conflagration become inevitable. The Mountain man that attempts to redress the injustice of the law by using the rifle is no more guilty in his lawlessness than is the millionaire corporation that uses shrewd lawyers instead of rifles. Is he not really less accountable than criminal lawyers that for a large fee assist guilty clients to defeat justice?

"We're pore folks, and we cain't fight money in the courts."

"We hain't had much schoolin', and when judges and lawyers with heaps o' larnin' scrouges a pore ignorant jury, what can ye do?"

"Every feller has to fight with the weapons he can git."

The political struggle in such conditions is not prompted by ambition, but always by the craving for safety. The contest is not for congressman or legislator, but for the local offices of sheriff, county judge, marshal, constable, or jailer. These would be able to pick a jury of kinsmen, or issue warrants against one's enemies, or unlock the jail door to let one escape, or kill an inconvenient enemy while pretending to arrest him.

It was possibilities, nay, probabilities, like these that caused such fierce contests and such bitter feeling over elections. The election of one such candidate undoubtedly meant death to a good many of those opposing him—death by assassination, sometimes from ambush, sometimes under cover of the law.

A brief sketch of some of these conditions must suffice. Interested readers can find ample records of details of such strife in Mutzenberg's *Kentucky's Famous Feuds and Tragedies*.[1]

Tom Dillam, a wealthy land owner, married John Bohn's daughter, who soon left him. One day Mrs. Dillam angrily returned to her husband's farm and took one of her aprons from a woman working in the field. Dillam went to recover it, quarreled with her, and shot his father-in-law, killing him instantly. Dillam baffled the courts

[1] Published by R. F. Fenno and Company, New York.

for many years by shrewdness and intimidation. He armed and incited his relatives and friends till he had behind him a whole band of arrogant outlaws. In 1885, Bohn's son William had a dispute over timber with Tom's brother, George Dillam, who, knowing the band would back him, became insolent. Bohn armed himself with a Winchester and soon met George Dillam similarly armed. Both darted behind trees and began firing. Dillam was killed. Bohn, wounded, ran for shelter, but was killed by George's brothers, Sam and Curt.

One of Bohn's friends was now drawn into the feud, Lem Buffum. He had married a sister of George and Sam Dillam. But the Dillam band were bitter against him because of his former friendship with Bohn. There was a dance on Christmas night at which two of the Dillam band who had been drinking sought a quarrel with Buffum. Suddenly it blazed forth, and when the smoke cleared, the two lay dead upon the floor. Buffum fled to a neighboring state. His brother-in-law, Sam Dillam, followed him relentlessly. Once he grazed Buffum's head with a rifle ball. Again, reckless with drink, Sam taunted and threatened him. Buffum, suspecting an ambush, cautiously retreated, Sam following. When Buffum reached home, he turned, and as soon as Sam entered his lot, he killed him. Buffum wished to surrender to the officers, but neither they nor the courts would protect him. That would be merely to invite assassination, unarmed.[1]

The Dillams began a reign of terror. They threatened every Buffum sympathizer, riddled their houses with bullets or killed them outright. Buffum's aged mother was conveyed across the river by Jack Smith, who was thereupon waylaid and killed. Jake Kimbrell, another friend, was seized at a dance and held fast while one of the band killed him.

But they were carrying things too far. Ab Dillam, a brother of Tom, would not help to hunt Buffum. Ab's son, Jesse, had married Buffum's sister. In his absence, his house was riddled with bullets, but his wife and children escaped. The camp of civil engineers surveying for a new railway was raided. Nobody was safe. The Governor, when asked for troops, refused to send them, because the sheriff had not made any attempt to capture the murderers with a posse of citizens. But the citizens knew that unless they killed or captured all the outlaws, their families would be attacked, their homes burned, and they themselves constantly ambushed.

The judge called for fifty militiamen; fifteen responded. With this puny force, the sheriff started out. A lad on horseback saw the officers and gave the alarm. The outlaws escaped into adjacent

[1] Once when the circuit court was in session, Tom Dillam and his band entered, broke up the court, and ordered the Judge to leave the county.

hilly woods. The sheriff retreated, fearing an ambush. He left seven men at Jesse Dillam's house to guard it till Jesse could move his family to a safe distance. Within an hour they were surrounded, the outlaws creeping close through high corn. Jesse sent away his wife and children, and all started for a neighbor's log house, which would better resist attack. They never reached it. One was killed instantly, one fled, and the rest, badly wounded, managed to escape. The outlaws planned an attack upon the county seat, where the wounded men were, but the activities of the sheriff deterred them. Various attempts at arrest were, however, futile.

Circuit Court soon met, and Tom and Curt Dillam were arrested, but Tom was released on $5,000 bail. Thus have Mountain courts, badgered by unscrupulous lawyers, "protected" innocent citizens from desperadoes. Some weeks later Tom Dillam was walking toward the courthouse with his lawyer, followed by his lieutenant and another man. When opposite the house where their wounded victims were, they started across the street, drawing their pistols. The lawyer fortunately walked on. The outlaws had scarcely reached the middle of the street when a terrific fire poured upon them. Tom Dillam fell, pierced by sixteen bullets. Jesse Dillam, Buffum, and their friends had been secretly warned and were ready.

WHEN A ROAD ISN'T A ROAD

This creek-bed is the only road there is in the district. When there are only a few inches of water in it, one can easily "ford it eendwise," but "when it is swollen with melted snow, you wonder with each step whether your horse has found bottom or whether he will slip on a submerged boulder and throw you over his head."

THE SECRET OF THE FUTURE

One of the Mountain schools, with the help of the neighbors, developed a strong sentiment for better roads, and several hundred men came to a "working." Right of way was given through tillable fields so that the road could be "carried back from the creek" to higher ground.

With the death of Tom Dillam, people breathed more freely. But the poison, of course, had entered into the fabric of the community. Accustomed so long to no constraint of law or duty, these men grew brutally arrogant and cruel. Tom Dillam's son, now the leader of the band, wishing to remove a rival, gave one of his band twenty dollars and a gun to kill him. The slyest of the band planned the murder. He knew that a young woman had invited the victim to supper on a certain evening. Accordingly, he also secured an invitation from the young woman for that same evening. While the party was gathering around the dining-table, he slipped back into the parlor and pinned back the heavy window curtains. After supper the victim stepped into the parlor and was instantly shot by someone outside the window. The community was indignant, and the criminals were hunted down; some of them were killed, the rest were captured.

But even when such flagrant criminals were captured, punishment was not at all certain. Curt Dillam was released on bail, but his body was found shortly after in the woods. Doubtless he was shot by someone who was disgusted with "the law's delays" and afraid that the released outlaw would seek vengeance on those that had given testimony against him.

A more famous feud was known as the Rowan County trouble.[1]

[1] Condensed from Mutzenberg.

In 1874, Thomas F. Hargis, Democrat, Captain in the Confederate Army, was a candidate for Circuit Judge against George M. Thomas, Republican. Opponents said Hargis was not old enough as a man or as a lawyer to be eligible. Hargis went to his former home in Rowan County to get the court records. The pages had been cut out. The campaign became very bitter. Hargis was defeated. Two years later he was elected. In 1879 he ran for Appellate Judge of Kentucky. In spite of great opposition in the Democratic Convention he was nominated and later elected. Newspapers had persistently circulated virulent accusations and counter-charges. In Rowan County the division was sharp. Voting at that time was not by secret ballot, but was public, the voter's name and his choice being called out aloud. This made it possible to buy votes and see that they were cast as agreed. Bribery became very common, and as whiskey was permitted everywhere, fights were frequent.

These conditions grew worse year by year. In 1884 a close race for Sheriff between Cook Humphrey, Republican, and S. B. Goodman, Democrat, fanned the coals into a blaze. In a general fight one man was killed and two were wounded. Sizemore was supposedly wounded by Sheriff Day, and Martin by Floyd Tolliver. The Martins and Sizemores, the Days and Tollivers organized and armed. A few months later Martin met Floyd Tolliver in a saloon. Flushed with liquor, they quarreled, and Tolliver was killed. Martin was lodged in jail, but the court, fearing violence, transfered him to Winchester. The Tollivers were furious. Instead of sending for Martin for trial, the Judge postponed the proceedings lest the Tollivers assassinate the prisoner on the journey. The town marshal, a Tolliver clansman, took four others, and, with a forged order, got Martin from the Winchester jail. The train was stopped at a flag station, a band of Tollivers entered and killed the handcuffed prisoner. The County Attorney had incurred Tolliver hostility by taking the prisoner to Winchester. He was now accused by the Martins of conniving at this murder. He was shot from ambush and severely wounded, whereupon he left the county and settled elsewhere.

A few weeks later, at the same spot, Deputy Sheriff Baumgartner was shot and killed presumably in retaliation by the Tollivers.

This gave rise to a battle in the streets of Morehead. Sheriff Humphrey, the Martins, and H. M. Logan occupied the Carey Hotel; the Tollivers, Days, and Bowlings gathered at the Cottage Hotel. Continuous firing kept the inhabitants in terror for many hours. Though houses were riddled and splintered, nobody was killed. But the peaceable citizens left in large numbers.

The Governor sent the Adjutant General of Kentucky to Rowan County to investigate. On receiving his report, the Governor, instead of prosecuting the offenders, summoned the leaders of both sides to Louisville. Here they agreed to return home, lay down their arms, and keep the peace. This weak-kneed compromise was, of course, immediately broken. Pierce, the companion of Humphrey on the day of the battle, was arrested in another county for robbery. In jail he admitted shooting Young and implicated the Sheriff and a stranger, Rayborn. He also accused Martin's sisters of employing him to kill Young.

The accused denied the charge and said Young had bribed Pierce to make the confession. But though unproved, this added fuel to the flame. The Tollivers kept a constant watch upon the Martin home about a mile from Morehead. In July two men were reported there. Craig Tolliver, Bowling, Day, and others surrounded the house all night, and next morning forced their way past the women to the stairway, where Tolliver was severely wounded with a shotgun. He was sent to Morehead, and from there directed a lot more to help in the attack from every side. Twenty-five or thirty assailants fired into the house all day. Humphrey and Rayborn realized that when night fell there would be a rush from all sides, in which the women would almost certainly be killed. Both men ran out in the hope of drawing away the attack, but Rayborn was killed. Humphrey, on the other hand, miraculously escaped. The Tollivers then set fire to the house, the women still in it. Unnoticed, however, they managed to escape, delaying only long enough to build with fence rails a pen over the body of Rayborn to protect it from hogs or dogs. These women swore out warrants against Craig Tolliver, Bowling, and others, but the examining trial was a farce.

A lull occurred for a time, in which Wiley Tolliver was killed in a drunken squabble and a man named Pelfrey was killed by Tom Goodan, Wiley's brother-in-law. Goodan was tried, but acquitted.

As election day drew near, Humphrey and Craig Tolliver roamed through the County with armed followers. On court day the new sheriff attempted to arrest Humphrey. Firing became general, the sheriff and his son were wounded, and a young son of H. M. Logan was killed. State troops were demanded. They were ordered out and remained for several weeks, and the election passed without bloodshed.

At the next court a prosecuting attorney appointed from Louisville recommended another compromise because he felt that it would be impossible to secure impartial trials. Humphrey and Craig Tolliver signed agreements to leave

Rowan County forever. With Humphrey's departure, the Martin faction disbanded. Tolliver returned in twenty-four hours, and, with his followers, became more insolent than ever. Magistrates that were not Tolliver partisans were intimidated, and violence went unpunished. To any protesting citizen Craig Tolliver sent a written notice of his funeral on some early date. Many left; others, who disregarded the notices, were murdered. Among the latter was the Constable, Keeton, killed by Bud Tolliver. Howard M. Logan, after being wounded from ambush, left the county. Judge Carey's hotel was shot almost to pieces. He left. Of the seven hundred inhabitants of Morehead, four hundred left. Craig Tolliver elected himself police judge and Bunk Mannin, town marshal. The Tollivers now controlled all the machinery of the law. When two daughters of Howard M. Logan were courageous enough to testify against the Tollivers before the grand jury, they were immediately indicted for perjury. Mrs. Martin was indicted for sending a poisoned turkey to a Tolliver partisan. Dr. Henry S. Logan, his sons William H. and John B., with others, were arrested for conspiring to murder. They were lodged in jail at Lexington. The sons gave bond and returned to look after the farm about four miles from Morehead. Another indictment was issued against the boys, and Judge Craig Tolliver, Bunk Mannin, and ten other men went to arrest them. In this posse were Deputy Sheriff Hogg, Bud, Jay, and Cal Tolliver. They set fire to the house, murdered the boys, and trampled them beyond recognition.

Next day, Daniel Boone Logan, a cousin of the boys, with two friends, took up the bodies for burial. That night they received notice that if they attended the funeral, they would be treated in similar fashion. Boone Logan was commanded also to leave town. Craig Tolliver wrote that he would rent Logan's house and hire out Mrs. Logan to make a living for her children. Boone Logan tried in vain to get the murderers arrested. He then, in secret meetings, got a number of men pledged to bring about the Tollivers' arrest and trial. Logan was chosen leader. He decided to go to Frankfort and ask the Governor for troops. In case this was refused, he had another plan. For a week he continued making his preparations, while the Tollivers made futile search for him, patrolling every road, even searching the outgoing trains. Logan eluded the Tollivers and reached Frankfort. The Governor, taking refuge behind a technicality, refused to help. He would neither send troops nor lend arms. Logan felt the hopeless impotence of the enslaved. The whole machinery of justice was either corrupt or paralyzed. At that very moment his wife and children might be murdered. What could a law-abiding man do? With eyes that blazed, he looked into the eyes of the official. "Governor, I have but one home and but one hearth. From this I have been driven by these outlaws and their friends. They have foully murdered my kinsmen. I have not before now engaged in any of their difficulties —but now I propose to take a hand, and retake my fireside or die in the effort."

Logan went to Cincinnati, bought several hundred dollars' worth of rifles, pistols, shotguns, and ammunition. These he boxed and shipped as saw-mill fixtures to a little station some miles from Morehead. Logan returned to Morehead, summoned his friends (many came from neighboring counties), supplied them with arms, and gave Sheriff Hogg the legal warrants for the arrest of the Tollivers. The citizens were to act only if the Tollivers resisted arrest. They closed in around the town in various bands. Logan was stationed near the depot, Pigman across the road with a half a dozen more.

As might have been expected, Hogg failed them. The Tollivers discovered the plan and began a furious attack. Having waited for the Sheriff as long as they dared, Logan's forces began firing in return, and the battle soon raged wherever his followers were stationed.

Craig Tolliver and his kinsmen were driven to the Central Hotel. Logan, exposing himself to the fire of these concealed enemies, ceased firing and demanded their surrender, promising them protection. They refused, and the firing continued until Craig Tolliver and the other leaders were killed. The battle lasted two hours. As soon as the firing ceased, a public meeting was called. People, relieved that the dreaded Tollivers were wiped out, flocked to it. A Law and Order League was formed, and armed men were appointed to patrol and guard the town until the troops again demanded should arrive.

"For the first time in many months the town was quiet. The yells and defiant curses of drunken desperadoes were heard no more."

From these examples, it is evident that: no feud could arise if the courts were above suspicion, and the people could trust themselves to them; if the courts were reasonably certain to punish criminals, and to punish promptly; if the community felt that justice would be done impartially and fearlessly; if witnesses felt secure in giving testimony, and jurymen knew that they would be protected from private vengeance.

This situation is part of the great national problem of the deplorable inefficiency and perversion of the courts of law. All of America has been settled and built up by successive migrations beyond the jurisdiction of constituted authority. Naturally, therefore, one element in the American spirit—where not yet purged out—is a boyish sense of irresponsible freedom when playing truant in the woods. In the untraveled isolation of the Mountains, this somewhat insolent sense of freedom has remained a little longer and a little stronger than elsewhere.

A study of the examples of feuds cited above will show that while there is in the blood of the Mountain People a tendency to clannishness and exaggerated family loyalty, there is no such thing among them as clan organization or clan government, as is asserted by some writers. In the first case, a brother of the Dillam leader remained neutral, until he and his family in self-defense turned *against his own kin,* or clan, as these writers would term it. In the other case, Boone Logan had remained neutral almost to the last, and various others were drawn in, one at a time, but always *by personal circumstances.* Their kinship was undoubtedly one factor in their being drawn in, but others just as close in kinship were not drawn in. If there had been clan organization or clan government, the whole connection would have arisen at once. As a matter of fact, in many instances the "band" that a feud leader has gathered has been largely of mercenary origin, though doubtless there has often been more or less remote kinship between these hired feudists and their leader.

A word of caution should be added before leaving the subject. The feudists have never constituted more than a very small proportion of the people. Why then, someone asks, did not the majority arise and put a stop to the feud? How could they arise? Some one person would necessarily have to stir folk up and organize them. But he would be shot before he could rally people together. Even if he escaped assassination, what do you think he could do? What do you mean by "arise"? Do you want him to arm the good citizens and put down the feud by force? Then he and his followers would themselves be unlawfully under arms, and disturbers of the peace. Oh, no! You want them to put it down by the ballot. It may be eighteen months till the next election. When that time comes, what hope? Under our American system of government, the few men that control the party machinery have the rest of us by the throat. If those few men are determined lawbreakers, what can be done?

There must be vigorous agitation and free discussion, and an expensive and skilful political campaign must be started. But when the few men in control of the political machinery mark for assassination any man that starts such a campaign, the average individual decides to mind his own business. This, of course, is not the ideal of patriotism. But how far does it differ from the action of other communities with far greater opportunities for enlightenment and burdened with no such handicaps?

There are many Mountain men still living that

have fought in a feud. Some of them are brutal and murderous gunmen, others are peaceable gentlemen, most desirable citizens, comparable to our Revolutionary fathers, who took up arms only as a last resort.

While there are a good many places where a feud might even yet blaze forth from the old smoldering embers, such an irruption is not probable. The feud cannot stand against genuine freedom of speech and the community spirit.

The conditions that made feuds possible are rapidly passing away. Almost everywhere they have already largely passed. Outsiders have moved in, or Mountain men from other counties who are unconnected by kinship. Some of the younger men have been away to school, where they have learned to think and act for themselves. With such men in the community, the favorable verdict of public opinion cannot be so securely assumed by the partisan leaders. The solidarity broken, the coercion of kinship becomes much weaker, and the invisible rule gradually fades.

The Mountains Go to School

The Mountains Go to School

THEIR greatest need is good schools adapted to their conditions—schools that will make them intelligent about the life they live; that will teach them what they need to know to enable them to adjust themselves to their environment and to conquer it; schools that will appeal to children and grown people alike; schools with courses of study growing out of their daily life as it is and turning back into it a better and more efficient daily living.

P. P. CLAXTON

CHAPTER SEVEN

The Mountains Go to School

THE education of any community is more dependent than we realize upon facility of transportation and communication. Sparsely settled populations are never able to support good schools. Children from widely scattered families always have a somewhat ragged record of attendance. In pioneer places where sudden emergencies are constantly arising, the larger or more dependable children are frequently kept at home to help in this or that unforeseen need. Then, there is always a tendency on the frontier to measure one's ability by the practical tasks that confront every dweller there. The qualities necessary for success, or even for survival, are not those taught in the schoolroom. "Book-larning" is not of such immediate importance as skill with an ax and gun, courage in danger, and resourcefulness in meeting the severe conditions of pioneer life. In such a situation it is always extremely difficult to make schooling seem as important to the young people, or to their parents, as the competing activities that tend to crowd it out.

In the Mountains we have all these conditions existing at once. The isolation is accentuated. The people are cut off not only from the outside currents of modern life, but often they are unbelievably separated from "near" neighbors. Two families living on parallel creeks only a mile or two apart may be separated by a mountain, over whose shattered cliffs there is not even a path. Down near the mouth of a creek the people are waterbound whenever there are heavy rains. Even the agile and hardy animals sometimes slip on the wet mountain paths and break their legs or their necks. Slips or landslides are a constant danger in the rainy season. Every strong wind breaks down dead limbs and often large trees. How resolutely would you send your children to school in the face of these dangers?

Because of such conditions, there is in the Mountains a startling proportion of men and women that cannot read and write. But in frontier surroundings the term "illiterate" must not suggest mental deficiency. The English nobility of an older day, men of culture and administrative power, left writing to their monks, as they left forge-work to their armorer or smith. So in our wilderness or frontier life writing was of minor importance. Far back in the mountains there died very recently a man who kept a large store —indeed, it was in some measure a wholesale store—yet he could neither read nor write. But his mind was so keen and powerful that he actually invented a system of notation and kept his accounts thereby. It would be rash to call such

A MODERN PRISCILLA

Back and forth, back and forth before the large wheel, Susie takes countless steps as she spins the wool that will keep the family in warm clothing and coverlids. Her mother, sitting at her work, is spinning flax at a small wheel, turned by a foot treadle. This wool from their own sheep and flax of their own raising will also be dyed and woven at home. "Hit ain't so purty as the fotch-on goods," remarks the mother, "but it's a heap endurabler."

FIVE MILES FROM THE STORE

When she's "clean out o' bakin' powders, and has broke her needle, and wants a new dress," the "woman" takes her baby and a basket of eggs and rides to the little store five miles away to barter for groceries and "fixin's." "Them eggs gets powerful heavy afore" she gets through, because her baby is "restless." Little Hiram climbs on behind to ride a mile up the creek to the schoolhouse.

a man ignorant; it would be wiser to recognize in him an original creative genius. He had been deprived of the schooling that most children receive as a matter of course. When he was a boy, doubtless the total taxes from his neighborhood were not sufficient to pay the sheriff; naturally there was no money for school teachers. Even today do not so-called civilized communities build marble-stepped court-houses when their sordid schoolhouses are quite unable to seat all their school-children?

Before the Mountain people migrated into these Mountain fastnesses, they were intelligent and well schooled. There are extant a lot of petitions [1] sent to the Virginia Governor and Assembly by the frontiersmen of Kentucky when the community was organized as a far-off County or District of Virginia. These petitions were for the establishment of ferries, courts, roads, mill-dams, land-titles, and so forth.

Many of the petitioners lived, as one of them quaintly writes, "in an Extream of the said County in the hills and Mountains detached from almost Every community or opportunity of information." Yet most of them signed their own names. There were comparatively few illiterates in those days. Even though they were then in strenuous conflict with the wilderness and the In-

[1] James Rood Robertson: *Petitions of the Early Inhabitants of Kentucky*—Filson Club Publication No. 27.

dians, the frontiersmen made strong efforts to establish the means of education.[1]

Before the Revolutionary War Augusta Academy and Liberty Hall Academy (in Lexington) had been planted on the western slope of the Blue Ridge in the Valley of Virginia.

As early as 1780 the general assembly of Virginia voted a tract of eight thousand acres to aid and encourage education in Kentucky, which had been legally organized as a county of Virginia four years before. This land was used for the founding of Transylvania College.[2] In this same year a Presbyterian minister, Samuel Doak, on his own initiative started a private school on the Little Limestone fork of the Nolichucky River. This, three years later, was chartered by the legislature of North Carolina under the name of Martin Academy. The year following, 1784, North Carolina ceded the land that now constitutes the State of Tennessee to Congress. This left the

[1] In Virginia, 1755—"More than forty per cent of the men who made deeds or served on juries could not sign their names, although they were of the land-owning and better educated classes." BEVERIDGE: *John Marshall*, Vol. I, p. 24.

"The solicitous anxiety which discovers itself in the principal Inhabitants of this Country (the wilderness) for having Schools or Seminaries of Learning among them that their Children may be educated as becomes a civilized people." *From a Petition of the settlers in Kentucky*, 1783.

[2] "A fund for the maintenance and education of youth, and it being the interest of this commonwealth always to promote and encourage every design which may tend to the improvement of the mind and the diffusion of useful knowledge, even among the most remote citizens, whose situation a barbarous neighborhood and a savage intercourse might otherwise render unfriendly to science."

settlers therein without any responsible government. They were naturally indignant at being thus tossed outside the pale of civilization, whereupon they drew up a constitution and Declaration of Independence, and formed themselves into the State of Franklin. The legislature of Franklin issued a new charter to Martin Academy in 1785. Apparently, upon the dissolution of the government of Franklin, the school was rechartered in 1788. Seven years later it was chartered once more by the territorial government of Tennessee under its present name—Washington College. This academy on the western slope of the Allegheny Mountains was the first school of classical learning in the Mississippi Valley.

In 1794 the Rev. Samuel Carrick laid the foundations of Blount College, now the University of Tennessee. That same year Dr. Doak moved down the river a few miles and started another school which grew into Tusculum College. In North Carolina they founded an academy at Alamance and another at Liberty Hall, which later became the State University. The Rev. Hezekiah Bolch started a school near by which later became Greeneville College. In 1802 Rev. Isaac Anderson founded Union Academy which later became Maryville College. Of course a dozen academies in these wide-stretched settlements could educate but a few, and later, when the public school system started, there was no supply of teachers to man them. Year by year the situation grew worse, as isolation congealed education.

Today, of course, every district has a schoolhouse of some sort, in which a school is conducted in some fashion. But the schoolhouse, the length of the school term, and the teaching are too often, one or all, very inadequate.

Level land is so scarce in the Mountain area that it is usually pre-empted for the family garden, which must furnish the major part of the food supply. Even if it were not thus seized, schoolhouses would not be built thereupon, for it is safer to have the children higher up, out of reach of the sudden tides, or high-waters that roar in torrents down the creeks after heavy rains or melting snow.

The little schoolhouse, therefore, is usually built on a steep slope, one side set up on stilts. It is seldom fenced. Even more seldom have any shrubs, flowers, or grass been planted. It is to be used only a few months in the year, so it is made as cheap and ugly as possible, and its surroundings are unbelievably bare and depressing. There are no outhouses and no playground.

Such a schoolhouse is not always furnished with desks. Its blackboards are often worn colorless, and chalk is frequently lacking. Often there is no chair for the teacher, and the stove pipe is likely to rust down or disappear between sessions. The school term is often discouragingly short. A few years ago a three-months' school was very common. But for most of the pupils that seldom meant sixty days' attendance. The average attendance in the district was often less than thirty days. Where would you and I have been with only thirty non-consecutive days of instruction in a year?

Recent years have seen great improvements in education. Schools for five months are now as common as the three-months' school used to be. And though many districts have still only a three-or four-months' school, a great number have gradually increased the term to five or six months, and a few are heroically supporting seven or eight. The average attendance computed by counties runs from twenty days' attendance in a year to ninety. Ninety days of instruction out of three hundred and sixty-five is the highest *average attendance* that any county shows. Of course many individuals in the county may have been present every day the school was open, but there were doubtless some who did not come at all, and many who came irregularly, making the best average very meager.

Not only in such districts is the public school term lamentably short and attendance thereupon woefully intermittent, but in far too many cases the teaching is pitifully inadequate.

The time is not long past when, in many districts, it was expected that the teacher would give one fourth of his first month's salary to the influential trustee whose vote elected him. An original and effective system of teachers' agencies! County superintendents are still living who eked out their regular salaries by selling to prospective teachers advance copies of the examination questions they intended to ask the candidates for certificates. When with even such assistance the way was barred to pedagogical progress, there were other avenues. On one occasion two brothers appeared for examination. The older was alert and acquainted with the usual subject matter, the younger brother was ignorant and rather stupid. The examiner placed the questions before them. They sat down and wrote for an hour. When the superintendent's attention was elsewhere, they exchanged papers, signed them, and handed them in. The stupid brother was given a certificate and was employed to teach a school. The brighter brother, of course, failed; but he went into the next county, took an examination there, received a certificate, and secured a school.

On the other hand, it is impossible to appreciate too highly the faithful labors of thousands of teachers who, with poor preparation in "book-learning," but with a passion for intelligence and with natural ability to teach, showed a patient devotion to the children's progress which is above all praise.

In the remote districts it is very difficult to get teachers. Even where the school is not given to some of the kinsfolk of a trustee, it must usually be given to somebody living in the district because there is no suitable boarding place for a stranger. Even if a room were obtainable, an outsider could scarcely afford to apply for the position. The average or median salary, at last accounts, was rather less than $250 a year. Of course this does not mean a full year's teaching, but because of the overlapping of school terms, it is impossible for a short term teacher to supplement her salary by securing employment in another school during the same school year and there is no other work in the neighborhood for the remainder of the year.

It was really easier to get teachers when schools ran only three months, July to September, because college and normal school students were available during the summer months. Six months' schools are often taught by ambitious young men or women who can teach through the school term and then return to their studies at Christmas.

Much has been written about the evils of tenant farming; the hopelessness of improvement when the tenant expects to leave at the end of the year. "Making things do" becomes a settled habit. "What's the use?" becomes the motto of action, or rather of inaction. There is a similar deadening influence in these sequestered and fragmentary terms of school. A teacher could scarcely hope to educate public opinion to any unanimity within a few months. And even if it were possible, it would probably be dissipated during the long interval before the next school term, supposing the same teacher to be coming back, a rather venturesome supposition. There can be neither continuity nor permanence in such school work. In the interim the pupils forget all they know and their thirst for learning disappears. The parents become discouraged, the community mildly hopeless.

In other parts of America there are in most communities a number of forces that help to create public sentiment favorable to good schools: the Parent-Teacher Associations, the Women's Clubs, such men's clubs as the Rotary, the Kiwanis, and the like, the local newspapers, the church societies, and the literary circles. In the Land of Saddle-bags these scarcely exist. There is no common medium of discussion. The people gather together pretty generally "when the Elder comes over from Hickory Ridge to preach," perhaps the last Sunday of each month. A small shifting group, men only, mingles in conversation every Saturday at the store, whither they have come to do their trading and indulge in the luxury of gossip. Groups of the younger folk meet here and there at a frolic or a dance, but general conversation is not their object, and community affairs receive scant attention. There is no common vehicle, no fluid solvent for the easy dissemination of ideas throughout the whole community. Perhaps even the term "community" is a misleading name for the scattered people that live up and down the same creek, each family like a remote constellation, revolving in its own fixed orbit.

An important contribution to education is made by books. These are far too rare in the Land of Saddle-bags. Many of the old people cannot read at all. Many more can only painfully spell out whatever is important enough to warrant the trouble. Windows are few and small, so the average interior is Rembrandt-like in its richness of shadow. There is no reading light within doors during the day. At night too often the light is weak, flickering, and smoky. It is much more comfortable to sit around the fire and talk to the neighbors that drop in to enjoy the warmth, the glowing firelight, and the family circle.

But cannot the state educational authorities remedy this condition? The State Boards of Education have very little authority. The State Commissioner can conduct a campaign of publicity and expose in the State Report the shortcomings of any county. But who reads the State Reports? The Commissioner can use his personal and official influence, and doubtless he improves many matters by advice and suggestion, but authority is largely local. Each county is its own master. The County Superintendent, if he examines teachers and grants certificates, has more immediate power and influence than the whole State Board of Education. Even if the Board had large authority, it could do little until the states in which these mountain districts lie adopt the policy that *the state is a unit for education.* The school funds are usually spent in the districts whose taxes produce them. Thus a prosperous district can have adequate schools, but its poor neighbor can procure only such schoolhouses and teachers as its meager taxes will supply. This is a weakness that should be remedied at once. As ignorance damages and impoverishes the whole state, improvement should be undertaken by the whole state. There are hopeful signs of an awakening in some of these states.

Even when the State Board has sufficiently affected public opinion at large to secure advanced legislation, such legislation frequently remains a dead letter in remote districts. For instance, in a state whose laws require the seating of children so that the light shall fall upon their desks from the left side, nearly every school visited was disobeying the law, and the children were straining their eyes to read and write in the shadow. The public drinking cup persists in spite of state laws. Quarantine is regarded with the same tolerant contempt accorded a book of etiquette, and children actually broken out with measles, or even with small-pox, sometimes persist in coming to school. When the law is broken by such flagrant sins of commission, one can imagine how often it is ignored by sins of omission. Yet the State Boards are doing considerable, mostly through the teachers, with whom they can most readily coöperate. In most states the teachers must attend the County Institute, or the State Commissioner can revoke their certificates. Sometimes local trustees make it difficult for them to attend, and occasionally insist upon the teacher "keeping school" at his own expense an extra week to make up for the time lost at the Institute. The Institute in some cases is conducted by anybody the County Superintendent may select, and may consequently be an empty farce. But it is usually made a profitable occasion. The betterment of the schools is coming largely through the teachers.

The improvement of the teachers, in most cases their self-improvement, has made encouraging progress. But the aforementioned difficulties of congregating and communicating make even this step toward progress at present almost insuperable.

Consolidated schools have been built in a good many places, with consequent improvement in grading, attendance, and teaching. But consolidated schools can never be very common in the Mountains until there is a miracle of good roads.

Conditions such as these have always constituted the Macedonian call for the establishment of special schools, whether the frontier was in New England, Ohio, Iowa, or Oregon. This state of affairs in the Mountain region has appealed to a score of church boards and other patriotic and statesmanlike groups or individuals, and more than two hundred schools, orphanages, academies, and colleges have sprung up in response. Some of these have recently given way before the improvement of the public schools, so that now there are about one hundred and seventy-five schools, and an increasing number of community centers or settlements.

These "brought-on," non-indigenous schools show every sort of difference in educational ideals, purposes, and efficiency. They range from kindergarten to college. Most of them started as elementary schools, taking the place of the public schools that were not there, or were not fully functioning. Most of them still do very elementary work. Some of them, striving to do the greatest good to the greatest number, keep the pupils only till they have progressed through a few grades and then "graduate" them to make room for others that are clamoring for admittance.

Some have added to the teaching of the grades a year or two of high school, or of "normal," sufficient to enable their pupils to get a third-class teacher's certificate. About one third of them have developed into four-year secondary schools, fully accredited for college entrance. Most of these still have a graded school attached, which serves the larger part of their pupils. The majority of these academies are in towns of one hundred and fifty to five hundred inhabitants. Less than a score are in towns of five hundred to fifteen hundred people; less than a dozen in towns as large as fifteen hundred. These secondary schools generally offer the ordinary high school studies, with the addition of religious instruction. Their curriculum is further modified by the fact that most of them are boarding schools, many exclusively so. This lays upon the teachers the responsibility for the pupils twenty-four hours per day, and gives far greater opportunity to mold the habits and thoughts through recreation, work, and social intercourse. The boarding and dormitory life involves household and garden chores, done by the pupils, and calls for careful and constant supervision by the teachers. The students not only learn to work, but to enjoy work.

During the last twenty-five years an increasing number of these church and independent schools have consciously attempted some measure of manual training, sometimes of the simplest. The boys cut the wood and kindling, feed the horses, hoe the garden, and bring in water. The girls wash dishes, sweep the floors, and perhaps wash and iron the clothes. Some schools with a well-equipped teacher give instruction in elementary carpentry to the boys, and a little more or less systematic instruction in cooking is sometimes given to the larger girls. Few schools are equipped to give instruction in any but practical cooking, and this is taught as incidental to the necessary kitchen operation of the boarding department. There is seldom any gas, electricity, or running water available, so that a laboratory for a cooking class calls for ingenuity and constructive skill. In spite of all difficulties, however, an increasing number of schools are giving more adequate instruction in cooking, sewing, the making of garments, millinery, carpentry, blacksmithing, and the elements of agriculture. Adequate work in teaching mechanics or agriculture calls for such great expense both in equipment and operation that most of these schools naturally shrink from the investment.

The policies of schools differ with their differing aims. Few schools can maintain an experimental farm for pure instruction in agriculture. Some try to give systematic instruction while tilling the land to raise the milk, corn-meal, poultry, eggs, pork, and vegetables for the school kitchen, together with the necessary corn and fodder for the farm animals. Others give only incidental instruction. Their chief aim is to furnish *work* by which the pupils may earn a large part of their school expenses. There is great value in doing work promptly, thoroughly, and cheerfully.

But we ought not to delude ourselves into speaking of such work as vocational training. A standardization of terms is much needed. It would doubtless be humiliating to some of us at first, but it would be a great help towards honest and earnest progress. Household chores should not be called Home Economics. Garden chores should not be confused with a course in Agriculture. The term Manual Training should not be stretched to cover splitting wood, hoeing corn, or patching the fence to keep out the hogs. These are honest and important activities, thoroughly worth teaching. But pretentious titles will inevitably transform them into shoddy and shamefaced trifling.

In every community there are a few people that long for better schooling than the local public school can give their children. Such parents eagerly grasp the opportunity to send a boy or girl to these boarding schools established in an adjoining county by some "good women," or to "Professor So-and-so's college," the latter being a "collection," not of buildings nor of teachers, but of pupils. The problem before the teachers of these schools is stupendous, and it is the greater because each school is facing it alone. There has been almost no concerted action. Educators in the most favored places are sometimes appalled by the magnitude of their task. We hear everywhere the complaint that the schools do not fit pupils for actual life, that there is too great a gulf between the sheltered school and the work-a-day world. How much wider must the gulf be when the world is a century further away?

It is evident to the thoughtful observer that a city-made curriculum is a poor sort of education to foist upon people that are rural, intensely rural, rural almost beyond description. On the other hand, what is needed is not training to fit and shape them to their rural habitat, but true education, individual personal development, which will prepare them for any enviroment by teaching them to know thoroughly their present environment and how to make it serve ideal and spiritual purposes.

The people that are teaching in the Mountains are divided in opinion as to what the program of education should be. This difference seems, however, to be virtually the same difference that exists elsewhere. The advocates of traditional education claim that it makes for culture and the richest use of leisure. Their opponents insist upon training people to perform easily and efficiently all the ordinary work of the world. But generally speaking, the training so far has been only for the kind of work found in cities. There has been little or no training for rural work and rural life.

The curriculum that has held the recognized place in American schooling was founded upon the *city* civilization of Greece, and the *city* civilization of Rome. It is a *citified* education, and is admirably framed to draw young people away from the country into city life. There has been up to the present no curriculum adapted to rural schools that has won wide acceptance.

It might, therefore, be naturally expected that most of the cultured people coming into the Mountains to teach would unconsciously use the same methods and the same material to which they were themselves accustomed. This material and these methods, even with individual minor adjustments, are poorly adapted to the super-rural conditions in the Mountain area. They either urge the Mountain pupil away from the Mountains or overwhelm him with hopeless discouragement. In either case they unfit him to remain at home.

Other teachers, in a reaction from all this, advocate training the Mountain student to fit him for his life conditions. But who is to decide what his life conditions are to be? What right have we to decide that he must remain forever in the Mountains? Training makes a man more efficient, but it tends to make him more of a machine. The fundamental difference between training and education lies just here. To train a man is to fit him for a definite task, to make a specific article, to carry through a certain process. The manufacture is the important thing, the man is incidental to it. The trainer does not ask what is best for the man, but what is best for the business. Education, on the other hand, cares first of all for the man, the woman, the child. Its aim is to develop him to his best, to help him to his full growth, to awaken every aspiration of which he is capable, to arouse every energy in him. The supreme aim of education is to create or develop a complete, well-rounded, joyful personality, sensitive to every aspect of his multiplex environment. Education is not principally interested in manufacture, commerce, or the bread-and-butter arts. Of course every man must earn his living, but after all, bread-and-butter is only secondary. If a man learns and masters his environment, he has mastered the provision problem and a great deal more. Education must fit him for the whole of life, and not merely for the procuring of food and raiment.

A man's joys must always be procurable from his present environment, his ideals must always come from beyond it. The rainbow's rim must always be a little behind his horizon. A little! But in the case of the Mountaineer, if the gulf is to be bridged, the foot of the rainbow will be not a little, but a long way beyond his present horizon. Very few of these schools feel quite sure that they know how to fit their students for any place that life may call them to occupy. For Mountain men are found in every state of the Union, filling important positions, with notable ability.

But you say that these are the exceptions, that

we ought not to shape our educational program for them. Let us grant the point. Yet ought we not to prepare the pupils to occupy just as important positions within the Mountains? And if there are no such places because of backward conditions, should we not so help to develop the communities that in the advancing civilization or socialization such positions will emerge? The unusual situation in the Mountains doubles the task educationally, but it does not release us from obligation. We must devise education not only for the boys and girls, but also for the community. Too many schools and colleges have eyes only upon the students admitted into their halls. They feel no responsibility toward the community, no obligation toward those unable to pass their entrance examinations. They are aware of the community only as a place whence they may gather their pupils. The great need of an undeveloped people, of a pioneer community, is a thoroughgoing school that keeps its eyes upon the whole community, not merely upon those that manage to scramble to its campus.

The gravest educational problem in any community centers about those not quite able to make their grade, those not able to pass the examinations in the eighth grade, or high school, or college, or medical, or law school, as the case may be. We have done the easiest thing when we furnish instruction merely for the eager and ambitious young people, who would go ahead in some fashion even without our help.

The school, like the church, should minister to the whole community in everything that tends to growth, to learning, to self-improvement, to bread, beauty, truth, and brotherhood. A number of schools in recognition of this community need have established extension departments, or have at least provided an extension worker.

In the majority of cases the term "extension" does not mean what those familiar with extension classes elsewhere would suppose. The conditions of travel, or more accurately of non-travel, in the Mountain area, preclude large or regular groups of extension classes. An extension worker could not visit class groups twice a week or even twice a month. Two visits a year are more than many extension workers achieve. This precludes the organization of classes, and reduces extension work to more or less irregular and intermittent lectures.

With all his equipment in saddle-bags, an extension lecturer rides twenty or thirty miles through mud and rain. After a hospitable supper, he addresses a little group who have gathered to hear the "speakin'." He speaks on the importance of good roads, or better schools, or pure-bred hogs and cows, or the value of legumes and clovers in improving the soil. Perhaps he has a set of small charts or pictures to show the con-

The Mountains Go to School

ditions of good health and the inroads of disease. Occasionally he manages to carry a tiny stereopticon and throws pictures on a borrowed sheet.

Perhaps the most striking achievement in the field of education that has been seen in the Mountains in recent years is the Moonlight School. In 1911 Mrs. Cora Wilson Stewart was Superintendent of the Rowan County Schools in Kentucky. A woman living seven miles distant, who could not read, sometimes came with a letter from her daughter in Chicago, who had studied in a night school. Mrs. Stewart read her the letters from Jane, and, as the mother dictated, wrote an answer. One day the mother appeared with a new dignity. "I kin read now," she said. She had actually taught herself from a speller. A few days later, in the Superintendent's office, a man was fingering a book. Mrs. Stewart noticed him, and offered to lend the book to him. "I cain't read or write. I'd give twenty years of my life if I could." There were in Rowan County 1152 men and women that could not read or write. With Jane's mother in mind, it flashed into Mrs. Stewart's mind that elderly people *can* learn to read. And, by natural association of ideas, they can be taught at a night school.

In the Mountains, travel at night, even in good weather, is difficult, and in many places it is dangerous—except on moonlight nights. Moonlight nights! Why not see how much they could learn in the pleasant autumn weather, before the roads became mere quagmires?

The teachers of the county were called together, and the matter was laid before them. Every teacher volunteered to teach four nights a week for three weeks—of course without pay. They agreed to spend Labor Day making a canvass of their districts, inviting everybody that wanted to learn to come to school. On the fifth of September the teachers were all at their schools after supper. They expected perhaps a hundred and fifty would-be students. Twelve hundred came. Their ages ranged from eighteen to eighty-six. Only one third were unable to read or write. Of these, some learned to write their names that first evening. A Bible was offered as a prize to each person that learned to write a letter in the first eight evenings. During the twelve evenings of the first session of Moonlight Schools three hundred learned to read and write. One man of thirty learned to write a legible letter in four evenings. A man of fifty did it in seven evenings, a woman of seventy accomplished it in eight evenings. A father and mother, with fourteen children and eighty-four grandchildren, both learned to read and write, and this gave great joy and new dignity to their absent loved ones in various states.

The next year, in 1912, two sessions of three weeks each were held in the moonlight of two successive months. Sixteen hundred persons

The Mountains Go to School

attended these two sessions, and three hundred and fifty learned to read and write.

During the third year, 1913, all but twenty-three of the remaining illiterates in the community learned to read and write. Six of these were blind or nearly so, six imbecile or epileptic, five were bedfast, two were new arrivals, and four stubbornly refused to try.

One of these four was in a district where there were 116 adults. The teacher, a young man whose home was in the district, enrolled 111 of these adults in the Moonlight School. This included fifteen of the sixteen illiterates. He had urged one old woman in vain. Now it happened that she was a "yarb-doctor." When the young teacher developed an eruption on his wrist, he went to her and asked whether she could give him some "yarb-tea" to cure it. While the mollified "doctor" treated him for erysipelas, he treated her for illiteracy, and she learned to read and write.

By this time twenty-five other counties, encouraged by Rowan County's example, had started Moonlight Schools.

Then in 1914, the Governor, by authority of the State Assembly, appointed an Illiteracy Commission for the State of Kentucky, the first in the United States. Very soon many states followed Kentucky's example, and an enthusiastic attempt was started to wipe out the five and a half million illiterates from the nation's population. Before 1920 over fifteen thousand illiterates in the Mountain counties of Kentucky had learned to read and write.

The Moonlight Schools in many places revealed a new community spirit, the spirit of intelligent cooperation. There was a remarkable loyalty in the teachers and an equally remarkable loyalty in the people to follow such unanimous leadership.

The Religion of a Stalwart People

The Religion of a Stalwart People

WITH all its limitations the Mountain church has been a conserver of the best in Mountain life, and is yet the best organized Mountain agency for the promotion of spiritual growth.

JOHN C. CAMPBELL

CHAPTER EIGHT

The Religion of a Stalwart People

THE Mountain People are unusually religious. Their religion, it is true, is not very dainty. It is the religion of a stalwart, independent people. If occasionally there is some admixture in it that might disturb refined appetites, let us remember that Cromwell's Ironsides also had some over-robust, not to say disagreeable, qualities, yet they were unquestionably devout and heroic men. No student of human nature will sneer at the sincere religion of the fierce men who followed Gideon or King David, the psalmist.

The Mountain man has an inherited conviction of God, a vivid sense of His management of the world. You would probably call him a fatalist. He bears disappointment or sorrow quietly. "Hit was to be, I reckon." His mind is still tinctured very strongly with the Calvinism of his foreparents.

These foreparents were, for the most part, Scotch Presbyterians from the north of Ireland. Mingled with them were smaller streams of French Huguenots, even more purely Calvinistic than the Scots; Palatine Germans, also vigorously Calvinistic; English Independents, a few Quakers, and a sprinkling from the Church of

England, the Mennonites, and the Moravian Brethren.

Almost all of these endured severe persecution on account of their persecutors' notions of religion. It is therefore natural that in the Mountains denominational lines should stand out strongly. These lines may not in these days be strongly emphasized in the community in which you live; you may even venture to cross denominational barriers and marry somebody in a different church. But in the Mountains, denominational antagonism is the survival of a life-and-death division. Its roots go back to the days of Queen Elizabeth, Queen Mary, and Gustavus Adolphus. In those days a difference of denomination meant being tortured or burnt alive, and the forefathers of these people actually suffered thus. So the slaughter at Drumclog and Saint Bartholomew's got into their blood and their vague but persistent suspicion of Roman Catholicism is an honestly inherited instinct wrought into all their ancestral memories.

Before the death of Washington there were at least a hundred and forty Presbyterian congregations in the Mountains. The mode of worship and church management of both the German and French Protestants was similar to the Presbyterian, so they readily joined with them.

In Virginia the Church of England, or Episcopal Church, was the established state church,

The Religion of a Stalwart People 193

supported by taxation. But the Scotch-Irish on the mountainous western frontier were so useful in repelling Indian attacks, and they were, besides, so far away, that their divergence from Episcopal usages seemed as unimportant as their other uncivilized wilderness ways. Many of their churches were therefore registered and their ministers licensed. Indeed, the vestries of established churches sometimes consisted wholly of Presbyterians. A church was established by the approval of the Governor, and the members of its vestry appointed by him or his counsellors. Thereafter, the members of the vestry elected their own successors. The Governor naturally appointed the men whose names were signed to the petition without very close scrutiny as to their religious opinions.

As the Revolutionary War progressed, the desire for freedom was strengthened, and increasing objection was made against taxing the whole people to support any particular church. So the Episcopal Church was disestablished in 1785. At that time many of the established churches in the western reaches of Virginia were found to be wholly Presbyterian.

But if the Mountain People were originally so unanimously Presbyterian, how comes it that today they are so overwhelmingly Immersionists?

Several factors have united to bring about this result.

(1) The very great emphasis the Presbyterian Assembly laid upon "thoroughly educated" ministers made it impossible to secure enough "thoroughly educated," venturesome, and comfort-defying men to supply the religious needs of the scattered wilderness dwellers. After long years of severe schooling, ministers acquired habits of settled study. A wandering preacher who carries his library in his saddle-bags, and whose study is anywhere "under his hat," seemed to the Presbyterians not to be taking his vocation seriously. It was a trifling with the profound and unfathomable mysteries of religion.

It was, therefore, difficult to find among the meticulously trained Presbyterians enough men of a rough-and-ready disposition to serve the growing needs of this wilderness ministry.

(2) The requirement of a long classical education, possible only by going a great distance, together with the lack of preparatory schools, made a native Presbyterian ministry impossible. No church can live entirely upon an imported ministry. Those denominations which ordained to the ministry the most suitable men to be found in the community, even if they could scarcely read and write, were sure to grow. Only such men, themselves born and bred among the hardy pioneers, could long endure the rough life of a wilderness preacher. And strange to say, their influence among the frontiersmen was greater

man for man than that of the more learned but less approachable college-trained ministers.

After the great awakening, under the preaching of Jonathan Edwards and George Whitefield in 1740-43, a great many uneducated men felt the impulse to preach and win men from wickedness. It was then easy to find able and enthusiastic converts eager to ride from one sparse settlement to another as the authorized heralds of the Cross. Their emphasis was upon experience rather than theory. Their theological tenets were of the simplest, and were quite definite, not to say literal. Their shrewd sense and rough sympathy, their ready wit and homely eloquence, made their "ap- pintments" a welcome event in every settlement. They felt at home in the rough surroundings and the unlearned settlers felt at home with them.

(3) There arose in New England, after this great awakening, an insistent movement in what was there the recognized church (Congregational) against admitting to church membership persons that were respectable but "unregenerate." Those who took this stand soon came, logically enough, to question the validity of infant baptism. These Congregationalists who wanted Christians to "separate themselves from the world," were called *Separates*. In 1751 the Reverend Shubael Stearns, with Daniel Marshall and a dozen fellow-believers, left Boston and went to North Carolina where by his great evangelistic

power he built up a church of six hundred members. His enthusiasm for a pure church, to consist only of converted members, was perhaps exceeded only by his fervent opposition to state control of religion. This opposition called forth a ready response from all Mountain men, whether they agreed with his "quar" religious notions or not.

The recognition of Stearns and of his co-workers as champions against the tyranny of the State church taxation probably accounts in part for the tremendous growth of the Separates. They were now as often called Separate Baptists as Separate Congregationalists, and worked shoulder to shoulder with the Regular Baptists in advocating religious equality and the disestablishment of the State church. Very soon after this division was accomplished, these two immersionist bodies united, dropping the words "Separate" and "Regular."

The Presbyterians had either been granted a large measure of religious freedom, or had quietly taken it, so that, not being in the teeth of persecution, they were not so noticeably identified with the clamor for liberty. Indeed, their possession of some of the established vestries, and the fact that certain of their ministers were licensed by the obnoxious opponents of liberty tended to align them, in the popular mind, among the aristocracy. In those excited years the sheer democracy of the

Baptist church government, the absolute like-mindedness of the rude preachers with their unlettered audience, and the vivid dramatic appeal of immersion made a tremendous impression upon the Mountain people. Since the Immersionists did not contradict any doctrinal teaching of the Presbyterians, their obstacles were few, and as their rough wandering preachers far outnumbered the carefully ordained Presbyterians, they gradually supplanted that less robustious denomination.

Turning to the religious situation today: If we take the circumstances into consideration, it is natural that the emphasis should be less upon the church as an organization than as an audience called together to hear a preacher. It is common to have preaching only once a month. There is very little church machinery. The preacher is the core of it all.

Though the theology of the preachers is severe and even harsh, it is frequently mitigated by a sense of humor, and the older preachers have often a gentle and kindly wisdom, distilled from their long service. Striking and memorable experiences are expected to accompany conversion. The sinner must labor under conviction as a preliminary. Then, after prolonged and sometimes intense wrestling in prayer, he "comes through," receiving assurance of salvation, preferably by some notable or strange token. "I prayed all night under yan plum tree, and at the first streak of dawn, I got peace, and afore sun-up, I tell ye, that old plum tree were jest one solid blowth o' blossoms."

The Mountain man enjoys theological debate. After a three-days' meeting at Macedonia Church-house, mostly a debate on predestination and free will, the discomfited preacher came over to see the Professor and get, if possible, some better theological ammunition for the next attack.

"I thort I had him, shore, Perfess'r. I said, 'If a man is drowndin' in the river and ye throw him a rope, he's got to use his free will and grab that rope, or he cain't be saved.' But that feller jest pounded the pulpitt and said that weren't no argy*ment*. 'If that man in the river was a corpse, dead in trespasses and sins, he couldn't grab no rope, without a work of divine grace.' "

This lucid counter-illustration evidently carried the day.

The attention of the Mountain People is largely caught by the mysterious or the magnificent. The unexpected approach of Death, the accurately detailed horrors of the Judgment, the somewhat sentimental satisfactions of Heaven, these are favorite topics.

They are fond also of texts that admit of ingenious interpretations. "Upon this rock I will build my church, and the gates of hell shall not prevail against it. That's the good old Babtis' church, the original Two-seed-in-the-Sperrit Hardshell Babtis' church. The Bible says John the Babtis' belonged to hit. And the gates of hell shall not pervail against hit.'' There is a mystical fascination in the announced topic ''Melchizedek, and the office-work of the Sperrit,'' and one's curiosity is not completely satisfied even after hearing the sermon.

Sermons are often delivered in a sort of monotoned ecstasy. This produces in many of the hearers a temporary semi-hypnotic state. There is little connection between it and their daily life. Their emotions may be powerfully stirred, but there is too frequently no issuance in action.

The old ignorant preacher who publicly thanks God because he cannot read, who prefers to open his mouth and challenge God to fill it with a message far more authoritative than that of book-preachers—this type is rapidly passing away. Now he is more likely to conceal his inability to read. ''My tex' air som'ers in the Bible. I ain't a-goin' to tell ye whar. Ye can jest read tell ye find hit. And ye'll find a heap more that's full as good.''

Outsiders going to a church-house in the Mountains to attend a meeting have been unduly disturbed at seeing people go in and out freely during the service. And they have been shocked at the unspiritual, or, shall we say, unrespectable conduct of some of the men, who apparently deliberately walk out of the church to trade horses under the shelter of a near-by tree.

To leave a service before the benediction is, of course, inexcusable conduct in a city church, where the pastor has been called with the explicit or implicit understanding that he shall never preach a sermon longer than twenty-five minutes.

But in the remote Mountain churches members have not exercised such sagacious foresight. Their preachers are not hampered by suburban time-tables. It sometimes takes them as long as twenty-five minutes merely to "git limbered up and goin' smooth." One can scarcely expect the sonorous repetends of rhythmic and resonant eloquence to unroll themselves in staccato headlines. In any case, the Mountain preacher is too independent to yield to the domination of the pew. And the pew would never dream of demanding it. Mountain folk believe in fair play. Let the preacher talk as long as he pleases. That is his privilege. Whenever any auditor has had enough, let him get up and go out. That is his privilege. There may be some people (evidently there are) that would be much annoyed if an influential committee stopped the soaring flight of eloquence in mid-career. Leave them to enjoy the eagle flight. Since the first preacher occupied more than an hour, and the second has just begun, go out and rest your wearied mind under a tree. You can go back for another spell of preaching later.

For there are three preachers sitting on the narrow bench behind the pulpit. And after each of them has had his turn, the presiding minister will ask if anyone else feels called to speak. If anyone does feel this inward urge, he ought, of course, to have freedom to speak. But it is recognized that the auditors also should have freedom, freedom to go elsewhere, while he disburdens his mind. If the preachers form a combination and "spell each other" in preaching, surely the people may also "spell each other" in listening.

There is a home-like simplicity in the meeting. A water pail is filled at the spring and set on the edge of the platform with a dipper therein. During the preaching, the auditors (especially mothers with little children) do not hesitate to go forward and drink.

When a convert wishes baptism, the congregation goes down to a pool in the creek. There is always an interested crowd, the older folk looking on with sympathetic approval, the young folk with alert curiosity. The preacher wades out till he finds "good bottom," then calls the convert to come down into the "waters of baptism," sometimes with stately and symbolic phrase. After immersion they go home without changing garments, unless someone has come a long distance, when he may put on dry clothes at a near-by house.

The "good old Baptis'" churches still practice

foot-washing. If the ceremony is to take place in the church-house, the church-members are invited to come forward to the front benches. The Elder (as they usually call the minister) takes the basin and towel and begins the ceremony by washing the feet of some of the men, they in turn washing others. The women wash each other's feet. Sometimes for this ordinance also the congregation goes to the edge of a near-by creek and the rite is performed with less ceremony.

It is noticeable that most of those participating are elderly. The members generally are on the shady side of life. Children and young folks can scarcely have had sufficient experience, in the heyday of their youth, to join the church.

Another fact ought to command our respect. These old Mountain preachers serve without pay. They work on their little upright farms, or in the blacksmith shop, or at "public works," like their neighbors, and earn their own living. Then they take the horse out of the plow, throw on the saddle and travel many miles to reach their "Sunday appintment."

One very obvious reason why so much of the preaching deals with death is the Mountain custom of "preaching funerals." The burial, of course, takes place immediately after death, but the funeral is "preached" in the early Autumn, when the weather is good, the cultivation of the crops is finished, the water in the creeks is at the lowest, and the kinsfolk and friends can gather for a fitting memorial. The chosen preacher takes the text selected by the departed, or, in the case of sudden death, a text chosen by the family. The choir, perhaps organized for this one occasion, sings the favorite hymns and perhaps one specially chosen on the deathbed.

The following words will give some suggestion of the awesome mood of the songs frequently sung at these services. But nothing can give an adequate idea of the piercingly mournful cadence, or of the quivering personal emotion expressed in the voices of the singers.

> O ye young, ye gay, ye proud!
> You must die and wear the shroud.
> Time will rob you of your bloom,
> Death will drag you to your tomb;
> Then you'll cry, I want to be
> Happy in Eternity.
>
> Will you go to heaven or hell?
> One you must, and there to dwell.
> Christ will come, and quickly too,
> I must meet him, so must you;
> Then you'll cry, I want to be
> Happy in Eternity.
>
> The judgment throne will soon appear—
> All this world shall then draw near.
> Sinners will be driven down,
> Saints will wear a starry crown;
> Then you'll cry, I want to be
> Happy in Eternity.

Another custom peculiar to the Mountain People is the "decorating" of burial grounds, a community celebration which has no apparent connection with the well-known memorial services for old soldiers. It is celebrated on any date convenient for the locality. The preceding day men meet at the cemetery to mow the briers, cut down the brush, and clean out the fence corners around the graves. The next day the people bring flowers to decorate all the graves. This done, the choir, having practiced for the occasion, sings the old familiar hymns, and, if ambitious, renders something resembling an anthem. If a preacher is present, of course he "improves" the occasion.

Religion in the Mountains, as elsewhere, is far more personal than public. "We shore ort to do what the Good Book tells us." "The Lord'll give us stren'th to bar whatever's laid on us, I reckon." "Hit's a sight how the Lord helps a body if ye trustes Him, Honey." And if the faith that an outsider hears voiced expresses more of resignation than of hope and joy, it is not the Mountaineer's religion that is at fault so much as the situation that bears so heavily and so unescapably upon their lives that in its clutches resignation becomes the primary Christian virtue.

Health and Happiness

Health and Happiness

NO Mountaineer closes a door behind him. As a class they have great restless physical energy. Considering the quantity and quality of what they eat, there is no people who can beat them in endurance of strain and privation. In spite of such apparent "toughness" the Mountaineers are not a notably healthy people. . . . That the hill folk remain a rugged and hardy people in spite of unsanitary conditions . . . is due chiefly to their love of pure air and pure water.

HORACE KEPHART
Our Southern Highlanders

CHAPTER NINE

Health and Happiness

"COME right in, Miz Lombard. You ketch'd me this time shore. I'm mightily tore up, and everything ontidy, but I'll find ye a chair.

"I been up the holler, sittin' up all night with Sally Ann's baby. Hit's jest a week old.

"Yes, mighty puny. Atter I'd studied on it consid'able, I 'lowed hit's head were sprung, so I bound its head with a cloth I tore up.

"Then I thought maybe hit were liver-growed. You don't know what that is? Well, you take the child by the right hand and left heel, and make 'em touch behind. Then I tuk the left hand and right heel and they wouldn't touch. So I jest pulled. The child cried mightily, but I knowed hit had to be done.

"Then hit looked hivey to me, so I gien it teas all night. Shore enough, agin mornin' thar was the hives out plumb thick.

"Hit's a mighty sick child yit, but with its head bound up, its liver let loose, and its hives out, hit stands a good chance to git well.

"I hain't had time to redd my hair. I had to pack my own baby home afore sun-up, and git the breakfast. I'm pint-blank drug out, but I shan't keer nary grain if Sally Ann's baby lives."

Good health is the basis of a sound economic condition in either an individual or a community. And a healthy economic life is the foundation for social and spiritual progress. It is true wisdom to scrutinize the conditions that affect a people's health.

Housing, food, and sanitation are not mere fads. They are matters of prime importance.

Log houses are comfortable and sanitary—if they are made so. The Mountain man, having threaded his way into the wilderness, naturally built his house of logs. In places remote from sawmills, the builder is still in pioneer conditions. Even on the outskirts of towns the man with little money today cuts down suitable trees, hews two sides of each log flat, notches the ends, and invites his neighbors to help with the house-raising. The corner-men fit the notches together as the logs are lifted or slid up to the top of the walls. After the top sills are laid, the rafters are put in place, and the owner can finish the house himself.

The space between the logs is filled with chips and stones plastered together with mud or mortar. A fireplace is built of stones, or sometimes of small tree-trunks lined with mud. If there is no sawmill near, the floor may be made of puncheons, trees eight or ten inches in diameter split in two and laid flat side up. Such a floor is rough and almost impossible to sweep. Such a house, built green, shrinks, warps, and sags. Cracks open everywhere, in walls, floor, and even in the roof. In winter one must draw the little hickory split chair close to the hearth, for most of the heat from the great glowing fire goes up the chimney.

The house may have a small window-sash immovably built in. Often there is none. The woman cooks breakfast before sun-up, and supper after dark, by the smoky light of a tiny kerosene lamp with no chimney. It is difficult to carry lamp chimneys long distances in saddle-bags. There are many homes where even the moderate luxury of kerosene is not found. A sliver of pine knot gives an even more smoky light, and occasionally a "ladle" is used. It is preferably made by a blacksmith, an iron saucer with a handle to hang it by. Narrow strips of cotton cloth, twisted or plaited together, are laid in the ladle in grease. The end of the rag is hung over the edge and ignited. Its illumination is not measured in candle power.

There are no built-in conveniences. A dried gourd hung on a nail will hold salt; another, sugar; a shelf or two forms the kitchen cabinet. Pegs or spikes are driven into the logs for the family wardrobe, besides which there is a large box, and sometimes a home-made chest of drawers.

During the day the door usually stands open a good deal, summer and winter. At night it is closed, and the room is occupied by an incredible number of persons. With a large fire-place, there is, of course, some ventilation, but where stoves have come in, the air becomes very foul. Even when, by adding more rooms, the one-room cabin has become a large rambling house, the people crowd into very few rooms. In a house having at least eight rooms, the wife and mother still has two double beds in her own bedroom, and this continues to be the family sitting-room, while the added rooms remain unused. No wonder a woman once said to me, "What we have a-plenty of is inconveniences."

Under such conditions, common cleanliness is often impossible. But even when the homes are scrupulously clean, there is seldom any knowledge of what constitutes sanitary cleanliness. They have no conception of the causes of disease nor of the means by which it is spread. This, added to a very common scepticism about infection and sanitary precautions, opens the door to typhoid, tuberculosis, trachoma, hook-worm, pelagra, and other insidious diseases. The sick and the well sleep together, and use towels, combs, and drinking dippers in common. The latter, indeed, are used also by any passer-by who stops for a drink.

The moment anyone is sick enough to be bedfast, all the neighbors come in and sit by the hour to show their neighborly sympathy. Quarantine is unknown and would probably be resented as interfering with personal liberty. Refuse and waste water are thrown out, to be carried away on the feet, or to seep into the near-by creek, and thus be carried to every family lower down the stream. The rapid spread of communicable diseases is thus to be expected.

Mountain People are usually very particular about the water they drink. They generally prefer spring water, and are emphatically partial to the peculiar taste of their own spring or well, be the taste that of sulphur, soapstone, limestone, freestone, or merely clear and cold. Like all other people that have not been educated in sanitary precautions, they do not consider water to be polluted so long as it is sparkling and clear. "Hit bubbles right out'n the ground, hit's bound to be puore."

The average cooking is bad and renders the food unwholesome. The frying pan is the most common weapon, though a stew-pot is a close second. In combination with the poor cooking, the restricted diet is responsible for a depleted physical condition. The range of foodstuffs is far too narrow for good health. "Bread" and "meat" are the staples of diet. This means corn and pork. The poorest renter or squatter plans to "raise me a crap" or to "raise me some bread" by which is always meant corn. And usually he slaughters a hog or two for his "meat." This, salted and sometimes smoked, provides the necessary supply of bacon, "ham-meat," and lard. A family with a supply of bread and meat faces the winter without anxiety. At least they will not starve. If further provender can be laid up, so much the better. They may "hole up" in the garden a pyramid of potatoes, another of cabbage, and another of turnips, and dig them out when the larder runs low.

Every family has chickens, but the hawks and the "varmints" (minks, weasels, skunks, and rats) get a large share of them. There are not many for the table. Eggs are not used so freely as they should be; too often they find their way to the store as barter for groceries, patent medicines, or feminine trinkets such as needles, buttons and thread, snuff and tobacco.

Milk forms a far smaller proportion of the family diet than one would expect, considering the fact that every family has one or more cows. But the difficulty of keeping milk sweet, and the habit of churning the milk (not the cream) every morning largely removes "sweet milk" from the dietary. Indeed the term "milk" usually means buttermilk.

A dietary meager in essential qualities and sometimes insufficient in amount lowers the vitality in many cases beyond the safe margin of disease resistance. Typhoid, for instance, is common and fatal. The high rate of mortality from this disease is no surprise when one sees that no precautions are taken against infecting springs, streams, and wells; that there is no protection

A "MEETING" AT WILDCAT MOUNTAIN

A "meeting" is always a religious gathering; discussion of politics, good roads, or community betterment is a "speaking." There is nothing cathedralesque about this "church house," nor about its order of worship. The "preacher" comes a certain Sunday in every month. He usually receives no salary, working on his farm or in the woods during the week, and riding long distances to his appointments on Sunday.

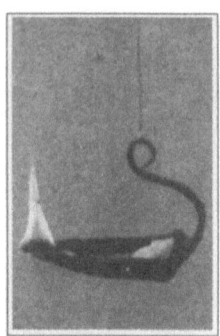
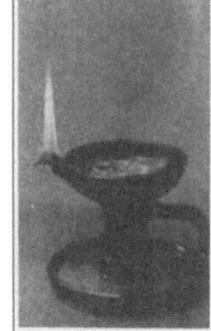

REMINDERS OF ELIZABETHAN DAYS

Like the customs, speech, and music of the Mountaineer, his dulcimer and oil lamp are survivals of an earlier period.

attempted against flies; and that body wastes from sick people are commonly scattered in the back yard or actually thrown into a stream.[1]

Tuberculosis is more fatal in the Mountains than in other rural areas, though less so, of course, than in cities. No precautions are taken because the nature of the disease and its propagation are not yet generally known. How long is it since the most privileged population began to understand this matter?

The reports of the Rockefeller Sanitary Commission for the Eradication of Hookworm Disease lay great stress upon the ravages of this disease in the Mountain region, and the great improvement that follows treatment. It is supposed that the hookworms are caught by going barefoot upon infected or infested areas. Subsequently the vitality of the patient is sapped, and his energy pitiably reduced.

"Sore eyes" is another very common affliction

[1] There are no authorized statistics available for what we are discussing as The Land of Saddle-bags. Its boundaries are not coincident with the political boundaries of state and county. The facts about the Mountain counties in each state are, of course, merged into the general averages of that state. There have been a few "surveys" made by non-governmental organizations. These usually cover one or two counties, and take account of only one matter, such as Child-welfare, or Trachoma, or Tuberculosis, or Hookworm.

Most of the states in which the Mountain People are located are vigorously working through their Boards of Public Health towards the improvement of the situation. Their Departments of Education are cooperating with the Health officers to disseminate information through the school children. It is a huge task, and the means of dissemination are few and slow-moving.

in some districts. Dr. McMullen, of the United States Public Health Service, directed a survey of twenty-three mountain counties in Kentucky. He found that seven per cent of those examined had trachoma. "The type of the disease found was severe, and its mutilating effects are seen everywhere. It would be difficult to appreciate the suffering and disastrous effects of the disease in Appalachian America without actually seeing these cases and witnessing the pathetic sights they present. Most of the cases have gone without proper aid, and many without any at all."

The lack of intelligent care in general is responsible for much poor health. Every school survey or community clinic reveals a deplorable number suffering physical pain or mental detriment from neglected teeth, adenoids, or diseased tonsils. But trained physicians are scarce, the distances they must ride are great, and the roads all but impassable except in summer. In the remoter areas physicians are seldom called. They live commonly at the county seat, perhaps fifteen miles away. If a physician is summoned by messenger, a long time elapses before he can reach the patient. It is a day's journey for the messenger, and another for the doctor. The obvious result of these conditions is that the doctor is not summoned until the neighbors have "tried everything on top side of the yearth" and have given up hope of curing the patient. Naturally when at last the doctor is called, it is frequently too late.

Mothers, as a rule, have no physician's care in childbirth. The midwives are ignorant, untrained in procedure, seldom licensed, and without the slightest knowledge of infection or sanitary measures. Pre-natal care is practically unknown. In one survey prematurity was found to be the most prevalent cause of infant mortality, and nearly half the recorded deaths occurred within two weeks after birth.

The babies are not wisely clothed, they creep on draughty floors and nibble at everything on the family table from fat pork to coffee. It is no wonder that there are many tiny graves in the cemeteries, or that many persons who do grow up are afflicted all through life with "a misery in the stummick."

Many physicians, educators, and other workers for community betterment are heroically attacking this problem of public health. Clinics by visiting physicians and surgeons at central points, district nurses, systematic information in schools, and county-wide campaigns by State Boards of Health, are rallying points for the countless unheralded efforts that are being quietly and constantly directed against ill health. Dr. John C. Campbell says that during one short clinic in a school which has been foremost in this work, there were 10 major and 608 minor operations.

The reports from the Department of Health of the states concerned show an increasing number of similar clinics in which the state, the county, and private individuals are heartily cooperating.

In some schools the Extension workers conduct a Farmers' Tent Chautauqua in several adjoining counties. The program lasts perhaps three days at each selected site. There are, of course, lectures on improved farming and improved schools. There are lectures also upon health, with an attractive exhibition of pictures and charts, and practical demonstrations by a uniformed nurse. Besides the general lectures, there are talks to women on the care of babies, maternity, and first aid in the sickness of children.

The Health workers of the Extension service sometimes have a rest-tent at the County Fair, where exhibits, talks, and movies on health are alternated with attractive demonstrations showing how to cook simple and procurable dishes for the sick and convalescent.

The County Teachers' Institute offers a great opportunity. To a well-equipped lecturer an hour on the program will gladly be given to present these matters of vital interest. Often an evening hour can be secured, and by tactful invitation the most influential people in the community may be gathered with the teachers to see and hear.

On more than one occasion the writer has been

invited to lecture in the court-house when circuit court was in session and the county seat was therefore filled with people from all parts of the county. The judge would suspend the court proceedings for an hour, and the crowd would always listen with eager attention.

If representatives of National or State Health organizations should offer their services to the local authorities and workers, they would generally be hospitably welcomed. The outsider that pushes in without reference to those that should be his hosts might as well save his time and travel.

In addition to the various campaigns of information just mentioned, a good deal has been done both for information and remedy by various schools and by church boards, sometimes with the cooperation of the local community or some organization therein, but frequently with merely passive non-resistance or curious observation. There are an increasing number of well-trained and experienced nurses settled on school grounds or at some convenient spot on the creek. These nurses usually have tiny hospitals in which they reside. When pupils are sick, they are removed to the hospital and, by observation and experience, the patients get a new conception of what should be done for the sick. The nurse usually visits all the homes up and down the creek and helps with the babies and sick people. After they have learned to trust her, she enlists the generous aid of physicians and surgeons from the nearest cities, and arranges clinics for the free treatment of serious cases that need expert attention. But these devoted women, scattered here and there, are merely showing what needs to be done in the Mountains. At this time the States and the Nation should arise and do the task.

Wealth and Welfare

Wealth and Welfare

"THEY was married this mornin'. Yes, they've got something to start on. He's got a nag and some corn, and he's got a bed, and she's got a bed o' goosefeathers, and he's been off at public works and yearned him a leetle money to git some tricks and fixin's for the house. Of course hit ain't what you'd call much, but hit's a right smart for pore folks."

CHAPTER TEN

Wealth and Welfare

EVERY Mountain problem, whatever other elements enter into it, is largely a rural problem. Eighty-one per cent of the Mountain People are rural, that is, they live in places with a population of less than one thousand. In Virginia the rural population rises to eighty-three per cent, in Georgia to eighty-five per cent, in North Carolina to eighty-nine per cent, in Kentucky to more than ninety per cent of the total population of the Mountain area of the state. In North Carolina there are in the whole Mountain area only six places with more than one thousand population, in Kentucky only sixteen.

When you see the word "rural," what picture rises in your mind? A white farm house with green shutters standing in a yard with great elms. Clumps of roses, peonies, and irises among the lilacs and syringas. A garden with delicious vegetables. An orchard with golden peaches and red apples peeping through the leaves. A pair of bay horses in the spring wagon, ready to take the family to the concert in the near-by town. The hired man bringing in two great pails of foaming milk. The dining-room shining with glassware and silver, the pink-edged china on the snowy tablecloth, the fragrance of roast beef, pumpkin pies, coffee, and some kind of cake. After supper everybody bundles up, climbs into the spring wagon, and away they go to the rhythmic hoof-beats of the horses on the smooth road.

But in the Mountains there is no spring wagon, no smooth road, often no road at all. Your picture is of the suburbs; we are in the wilderness. The secret of the Mountain situation is that it is far off. The needs of the Mountain People are caused by their remoteness. For practical purposes they are five hundred miles from suitable tools and implements, more than that from the ordinary conveniences of life. If you go away on a fishing trip into the wilds of Maine or Michigan, you do without many things to which you are accustomed. Yet you have with you an expensive and elaborate outfit selected with care. Often there is an experienced guide to stand between you and any real discomfort. Suppose you should lose your outfit and have to stay in the woods six months without any guide. Try to imagine yourself coping with that situation.

May I once more remind my readers that the area we are discussing is not constant? The building of a railway to a mining camp makes transportation possible to the narrow valleys through which it winds. This melts down the isolation, and before long, modern schools, ideas, commodities, and, most of all, markets, become a new element in the life of the people along the edge of the railroad. What we call progress begins to modify the ways, the homes, the wants, the pleasures, the outlook, and purposes of the people. They assimilate whatever comes in contact with them, and their own peculiarities are in turn merged into a composite, the characteristics of their pioneer inheritance combined with that of standardized Americans. As such modification slowly takes place, the area of the Land of Saddle-bags is gradually decreased.

This gradual change in the homes and habits of the people is exactly the same sort of change that takes place, and always has taken place, in every developing country. Whether we begin with Abraham or King Alfred or Daniel Boone, we find much the same stages of development. First they are pioneers, skilful hunters, and hardy fighters, that wander about and camp wherever they find a place that is suitable and secure. Then they gradually cease to be nomadic and become settlers. They can scarcely be called farmers yet, but they build a rough house, fence a spot for the garden, and clear a small field for breadgrain. They are still hunters, trappers, and traders. They are not rooted to the soil, but remain only a few years in one place, and then move on. They want elbow room and, as soon as others settle within a mile or two, they feel crowded and restless.

While these restless neighbors turn their eyes to the wider spaces, those with the strongest home-making instincts remain, and these gradually develop from mere settlers into farmers. Common activities begin to emerge—a store, a blacksmith shop, a school, a local magistrate, representing the majesty of the law, an informal and irregular forum, where common interests are discussed and decided. As a Mountain man shrewdly remarked, "Mixin' larns both parties." The amount of "mixing" that has been done determines what stage of social progress any particular district has reached. The interchange of ideas and the interweaving of activities tend to bring all sorts and conditions of men into a homogeneous and united people. Only where such interchange is interrupted or hindered do startling differences appear. The obvious remedy is to clear out the obstructions from the channels of social and economic intercourse.

This chapter describes the conditions in those districts where this clearing away of hindrances has not yet been done.

The Mountain people are contemporary pioneers, remote in the wilderness, living without any of the conveniences that you consider necessities of life. All their habits and activities are shaped by this isolation. Above all, their economic life is conditioned by it.

A city employment bureau registers some hundreds of occupations. In *not a single one of these* could a man earn a living in the Land of Saddle-bags. Stone cutter, mason, blacksmith, machinist, carpenter, wagon maker, wheelwright, veterinary, bee keeper, bridge builder, shingle maker, farmer, gardener, orchardist, cattleman, poultryman, hunter, fur-trapper, butcher, gunsmith, barber, dentist, undertaker, each of these the Mountain man must be *upon occasion*. None of these activities, however, constitutes a regular trade or occupation on the part of the Mountain man. Each is only the meeting of an emergency, an incidental part of the day's work. In general, each man repairs his own plow or wagon, shoes his own horse, splits shingles, and roofs his own barn. Yet in every community, in the course of time, one or two tradesmen emerge.

For ordinary farm laborers there is little demand, and, it should be added, as little disposition. The urge for ownership is very strong, and the desire to manage for one's self even stronger.

There are, of course, in every community some men that are not yet settled in life, and a few who have been unfortunate in their finances. Some of these may be persuaded to do an occasional day's work. Until recently they were paid, not in money, but in corn at gathering time—a bushel of corn for each day's work, or in pork at hog-killing time—five pounds of meat for a day's work.

In the Land of Saddle-bags it is still true that

there is no economic independence for women. In conditions where every family group is a separate unit, conducting within itself all the basic activities of life, there are very few ways by which a woman can earn a living, especially if she has grown up with no training for bold and original effort. Usually the first trade that opens for a woman is that of a household servant. Here such labor in the more prosperous homes is performed by orphans who have been "took to raise." In a civilization where everybody is a *neighbor* of equal rank and social standing, the position of a domestic servant is anomalous and therefore rare. Dressmaking forms a negligible fraction of the community's activities, like churning or baking; each family does its own. Nursing, or midwifery, naturally falls to an occasional stalwart "granny-woman," or to a resolute widow, for experience is the only teacher. School teaching is merely a preparation for matrimony. Unless a young woman has a father unusually prosperous, she must get married. It is the only economic position open to her. There is nothing else to do. Even unmarried widows are rare. A few strong-minded widows, especially if their children are old enough to plow and hoe, have courage enough to undertake life without the support of another husband.

Two thirds of the Mountain men own land. From this land they must get their living. In

Wealth and Welfare 227

most cases it is largely covered with forest. But if accessible, it is a culled forest. On the banks of the rivers and on the "forks" and creeks, which have sufficient water to float away logs, the best timber was cut long ago. Later, as the price of timber increased, a swath of trees was cut farther back from the stream, extending as far as it would pay to haul the logs before floating them down. As the price of lumber rises, and the sawmills pay more for logs, another swath still farther off may be cut. And on land already cut over, trees that were formerly rejected as not good enough, may now be cut for second-class lumber. Beyond this riparian area, there can be no lumber cut or sold until railways penetrate in search of coal, or until macadam roads are built. Wherever a railway has entered, sawmills have been set up, and the timber cut in all the area from which it pays to haul. With no roads, it is a comparatively narrow area. Well-built roadbeds would furnish arteries to take the timber from a limited distance on both sides of a railroad. Here and there a few miles of such road are being built. But so far as the Mountain People are concerned, lumbering has become merely incidental. They must now get their living from cultivating the land.

Very little of their land is level enough for cultivation. They cannot earn a living by raising bulky crops like corn, hay, or wheat. By spending a few weeks in the saddle, one may see thousands of Mountain farms none of which has as much as ten acres level enough for a mowing machine. Most of them have scarcely two or three. No corn planter, no riding cultivator, no wheat drill, none of the improved farm implements can be used. To think of people in such a situation competing with the Illinois corn belt or the vast wheat fields of Minnesota would be absurd.

There is a very large acreage where even the turning plow cannot be used. A makeshift, called a "hillside turner," is widely used, and the simple "bull-tongue" or shovel plow (occasionally the "double-shovel") does what plowing is possible. On many a precipitous cornfield the hoe is the only implement used from first to last. The corn crop raised thus emphatically by hand is manifestly not sufficient for the family income, even if sold in the highest market. But even if a bumper crop of thousands of bushels could be raised, there would be no way, short of an aeroplane, to get it to the market. People that really live off the Land of Saddle-bags must raise crops that can walk to market.

In riding to and fro we meet a flock of two thousand turkeys, the charter members of which have been driven thirty miles. The buyers start with a dozen bought from a farmer's wife, and buy up each succeeding flock along the road. The news travels, and at intersecting side-roads, he finds little flocks with their drivers, the boys and

THE WARP AND WOOF OF MOUNTAIN ART

In teaching weaving some of the Mountain schools are preventing the extinction of an old and honorable craft and encouraging a promising Mountain industry. Many girls are learning not only to card, spin, and weave the wool, but also to dye it, for most schools insist upon the use of home-made dyes. Patterns familiar to the Mountains are often of remarkable beauty.

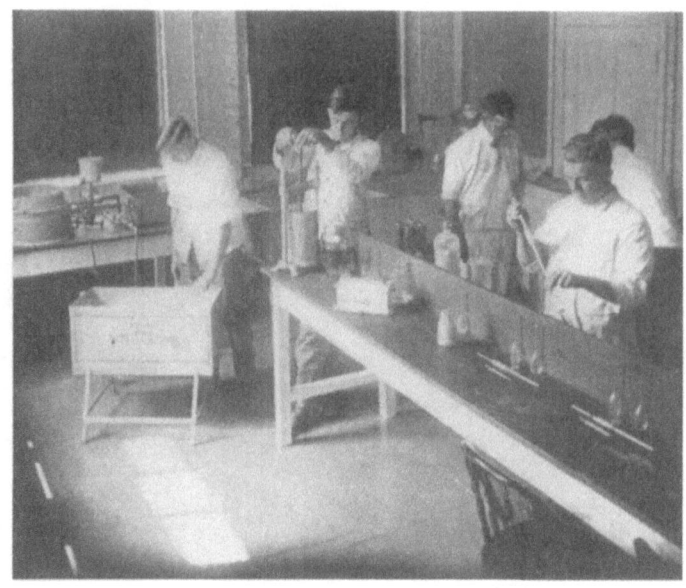

A CLASS IN CHEESE-MAKING

A few schools have equipment sufficient for teaching scientific and practical cheese-making of a grade meeting commercial requirements. Such schools help a people who "cannot with their bare hands cope with a civilization armed to the teeth with machinery."

girls who have raised and tended them in the hope of the money this peripatetic market would bring them. The gregarious instinct of the birds adds to the flock a good many that are not paid for.

Here is a flock of sheep that has come seventy miles—very slowly, for sheep are not good travelers. Later we come upon several droves of hogs, some in fair condition, others gaunt as greyhounds. Droves of cattle are not uncommon at almost any season. They are mostly yearlings or two-year-olds, the by-products of the milch cows kept by every Mountain family. The cattle buyers ride through the country at rather uncertain intervals and buy them up by ones and twos till they gather a large enough drove.

A few medicinal roots can be sold at the store, where a buyer comes perhaps once a year. Going "sanging" (to dig wild ginseng) used to be a common and profitable recreation which brought one a good bit of money as well as a pleasant ramble in the open woods. But ginseng has been practically rooted out. Fur-bearing "varmints" are trapped during the winter, and their pelts when turned inside out and dried on stretchers, are a recognized medium of exchange at the store.

Geese are very commonly kept, and their down, plucked several times during the summer, has a market-price at the store. Wherever a wheeled vehicle can go, there is a market for poultry. And these "hen-men" buy up the eggs and carry them over unbelievably jolty roads to the railway.

The egg-buying area is considerably enlarged by the women who, living miles from the store, clap the side-saddle upon the horse, and, with a large basket of eggs on one arm and the baby in the other, scramble up precipitous rocks or plunge down creek-beds that are half waterfall and half rapids, all of which are erroneously labeled roads.

The main economic problems of the Mountains are better agriculture and transportation. The Mountain family must raise more valuable products and must have assistance in building roads to get them to market.

An intelligent and industrious Mountain family, no matter how isolated, can raise most of its "living." It has a good garden, a flock of hens, two or three cows, an ancient sow followed like a patriarch by a litter of pigs, and a drove of shotes, a colony of geese, thirty or forty hives of bees, an apple orchard, a vein of coal at the kitchen door, a cool spring in the yard, and a flock of sheep up under the cliffs. With occasional rabbits, squirrels, and partridges shot by the boys, such a family is independent and comfortable. With a very small money income, they are prosperous. But how to get that small money income!

A great many try to get it by leaving home during the winter, or for several months in the summer after the corn is "laid by" (cultivated for the last time). They get pretty good wages at "public works." But the only permanently successful place in which to raise the income is the home.

The lean, leathery cattle must be replaced by pure-blooded animals of thriving and profitable breeds. It is not uncommon for cows to be out of doors all winter. In many places they find shelter under the cliffs, in the shallow caves or "rock houses" that abound by natural formation. Sometimes the lee side of a hay-stack is their only refuge. Even when there is a barn or shed available, its construction is frequently so loose that "it strains out only the coarsest of the wind." A primitive barn is quite commonly erected by building first a crib of logs. When it is six or eight feet high, four top logs twice as long as the rest are laid on. These form supports for the roof which thus extends not only over the crib but over a considerable space on all four sides of it. The ends of these long sills may be supported by posts. Sometimes this extra covered space is boarded up with split clapboards; often it is merely walled in with a fence of rails or left entirely open. Such a barn, when new, keeps off the rain and snow. But as the spaces between the logs are not chinked, it allows unrestricted ventilation.

The average cow gets some corn fodder and a few nubbins. She is left to get the rest of her sustenance from the scenery. In consequence, she is thin and uninteresting; so is her milk. Endurance is the chief characteristic of such animals. Cattle bred for other qualities—for beef, milk, quick growth, cheap fattening, or a great size—must have better shelter and better food.

More skilful agriculture must somehow be taught. Improved forage crops, such as clovers and legumes, must be introduced. Better seed selection and manurial values must become familiar matters. Then, with the worn-out hillsides put into grass and forage, more stock and that of a better kind could be sent to market.

I was visiting some time ago in a beautiful section of the Mountains where the people were unusually prosperous and intelligent. They had good schools, good churches, good farms, comfortable homes, good roads, and were sending a large number of their young people away to college. The valleys were not so narrow as in many places, nor the slopes so steep, but that was scarcely sufficient to account for the unusual prosperity. Had a different strain of people settled here? Or had some accident planted therein an agricultural genius? Or was the soil naturally so much richer that prosperity was the inevitable result? I spent some time investigating. Finally I found a clue.

"Twenty-three years ago, when I was married, there was not a house all up and down this creek as good as that one yonder." This statement was corroborated by unquestionable details. I at once set about finding out what had happened in the neighborhood about twenty-two years ago. After a good deal of questioning—because nobody had considered it significant—I discovered that a pure-bred shorthorn bull had been, rather accidentally, brought into the valley about that time. This was the unrecognized foundation of their prosperity. If we could put into every Mountain valley trusty breeds of beef cattle, fat hogs, and long-wooled sheep, the Mountain problem would solve itself. Or rather the Mountain people would solve it within twenty years.

But there are other obstacles to improvement besides lack of knowledge and lack of money. Personal preferences are an effective barrier, especially if the preferences are held with anything like unanimity. Enormous areas in the Mountains are favorable for sheep. But most Mountain men will not part with their dogs. They would not accept a flock of sheep as a gift on condition that they give up their hounds. A lonely hunter's affection for his dog is stronger than any economic considerations. A boy's devotion to his dog is as unreasoning and wholesome. The Mountain man's sentiment toward his hound partakes of both these feelings. This remnant of wilderness freedom left to him is dearer than mere money. He loves to run foxes, or bears, or even squirrels; and he will be loyal to what he loves at any cost. Economic forces give him no concern. The laws of supply and demand stand no chance against the likes and dislikes of an unfettered life.

But the pressure of more compact community life has produced changes in the Mountains as well as elsewhere. Here and there a man and his friends have started a creamery. These industries are running successfully and are exerting a strong influence in their neighborhood for better cows, and better cows involve better feeding and care. In certain sections cheese factories have been the means of re-making the community. Making grape-juice is a feasible industry, for grapes are easily and successfully grown in most parts of the Mountains.

These are exceedingly valuable means for economic betterment. They demand local cooperation, but not great capital nor great knowledge for their beginning. Best of all they contribute to the staple food supply of the nation. They do not depend upon a passing fashion.

The economic problem of the Mountains is fundamental. Primarily it is a problem in agricultural education. With that in process of solution we can with some hope work for good health, good schools, and good citizenship.

But many of the slopes are too steep even for grass. Sod cannot develop fast enough to hold the soil from erosion. All steep slopes should be planted with trees. Reforestation should be

Wealth and Welfare

definitely encouraged, not merely by creating State and National Forest Reserves, but also by instruction and encouragement specially adapted to men that own small tracts of land and have little capital. They must be taught practical forestry, not as it ought to be done ideally by a rich nation, but as it could be done by a poor hill-farmer.

For this, as for every other improvement, there are no sufficient channels or media of communication. A campaign of newspaper information would reach a very small number. Newspapers are not very common, and many of the people are not ready readers. Besides, few newspapers give much useful information. Someone suggests a campaign of four-minute speakers. It would take these speakers two weeks to get to their appointments. Button-holing a million people is a considerable undertaking, especially when they live so far apart and in such remote and inaccessible places.

But however difficult the task, the Nation owes it to the Mountain People, and to itself, to undertake whatever remedial measures are necessary.

Of course when coal mines are opened or factories are built, the whole economic situation is changed. Around the mines it is profitable to raise vegetables, eggs, and chickens, and in the factories women and even children are employed. There is, of course, more money in circulation.

But no one that has made any study of social economics will be deluded into measuring prosperity by the bank transactions. From hunters to settlers, from settlers to agriculture, the social transitions are great, but they are very gradual. The transition even from prosperous and businesslike farming to industrial life is always very abrupt. When the agricultural stage is omitted, the transition from the rough, untrained farming of the settlers to the complex conditions of industrial life is a perilous leap. An epoch of industrial development is always fraught with grave danger to the ideals and morals of the community. There is subtle and serious danger in any expansion in which the whole community does not actively share.

The hazard is less when great industrial organizations grow out of the community's own internal development. But there is unspeakable danger when manufacturing, mining, and other mass operations are thrust into a backward community by outsiders. They are conducted not primarily in the community's interest, but for the benefit of the exploiters. The Mountain People are suffering from the ruthless exploitation of large financial interests. These foreign juggernauts may have secured their coal and timber lands for a song, but taking money from those that have no special use for it is not a fatal damage. The deadly sin is the thrusting of a ferocious and devouring social system upon an unprepared and defenceless people. In spite of all our boasted modern progress, mining still remains the hideous, devilish operation depicted in *Paradise Lost*.

A Mountain man becomes a miner. He moves his family and a few household goods from the picturesque cabin in the cove or on the ridge to a desolate shack in the sordid village that has sprung up around the mine. He had not realized that he would have to buy all his food. A garden and cornfield had always seemed to him an inseparable part of a house. His cow starves as she roams at large. Milk and butter had heretofore seemed almost a part of the landscape. He can keep no bees for the honey. There is no acorn or hickory mast for his hog, so he puts it in a pen and tries to feed it on table scraps. This encourages waste in the kitchen. He has to pay even for water to drink. The life of nature, of which he was a part, has been torn from him, and, stripped naked of all he has been accustomed to, he might as well be in a dungeon. The vices of our industrial progress fasten their tentacles upon him and soon suck out his life. His children are surrounded by ugliness instead of beauty, their time is spent in idleness instead of the healthy-minded recreations of the woods and the educative family chores incident to tilling the soil.

When the nation is in the throes of war, the authorities are quick to assert the solidarity of the population. Every man, however remote, owes his service to the nation. But when the danger is past, they quickly forget what is equally true, that the nation on its part owes a duty to every member. If all the people must equally care for the nation in danger, the nation must care for all its people in peace. The nation has never done its duty to those that have neither the power nor the skill to compel it. It has left them to do what they could for themselves. The nation owes education, communication, and transportation to all its people alike. If the nation had done its duty in education alone, the Mountain People would have been ready for the industrial invasion. Indeed, they would have forestalled the invasion by their own industrial development. But with meager facilities for education, communication, and transportation, development has been difficult, and a self-respecting solidarity impossible. For the Mountain People, compact geographically, are scattered politically into the helpless minorities of eight different states. Even if their thinking and planning were articulate, they would have no effective means to express their thought in political action.

The Challenge

The Challenge

IT is this transition that should make the challenge to the Churches today. A people who for generations have worked out their individual existence far removed from the forward march of progress is bound to suffer temporary demoralization when modern industrial conditions change their whole manner of life.

The Mountains need today new leaders who are willing to face new conditions. There are modern problems to be met. The imperative need, and we must not delay, is to develop leaders among the people themselves, that they may direct all the forces—economic, educational, social, agricultural, and religious—to cooperate in shaping an ideal, wholesome, Christian, community life.

HELEN H. DINGMAN

CHAPTER ELEVEN

The Challenge

WHATEVER is done for the Mountains should be done at once. The industrial invasion dispossesses the people, breaks down their old standards and usages, and grinds them down into a poverty not only of purse but of living, which their free and leisurely existence heretofore has peculiarly unfitted them to survive. But whatever is done, they must do for themselves; it cannot be done for them; a regrettable number of the two hundred educational enterprises started in the Mountains by earnest and kindly people have failed or have had only fragments of success because the benefactors have, with generous impulses, given too much and done too much *for* the people. It is almost cruel to hint to such devoted workers that they have deprived the people of a God-given right, one of the inherent rights of humanity, the right of self-help. No race or nation has ever been *lifted* to a higher level. It needs the stimulus of an outside civilization, the contact with a people of more advanced socialization; but it must climb by its own efforts. Unless it responds to the outside suggestion and stimulus by the exertion of its own energy, any apparent improvement is only a rope of sand.

Further, we ought to recognize that the law of progress demands self-direction. The problem before all these agencies is how to assist the Mountain People to self-help and self-direction. Long-distance instruction must give way to object lessons and to personal suggestions given by neighborly people who know the conditions intimately and who really respect their less experienced neighbors.

Of course educators in the Mountains are no greater sinners in this respect than are the majority of teachers in other places. But we must learn to do less telling and more encouraging, less directing and more sharing.

The Mountains have suffered, of course, from the ruthless exploitation of industrial magnates who have bought up priceless coal lands, paying sometimes as low as fifty cents an acre. They have suffered also from an innocent and very kindly exploitation by literary folk who have considered them an immense reservoir of quaint and original material for interesting stories—an unfailing resource for a long time to come. Writers, mission boards, and educators have all too easily assumed that conditions in the Mountains are static. Because these people isolated on this inaccessible island of mountains have remained in practically the same condition, socially, educationally, and economically ever since the days of Daniel Boone and George Washington, it has seemed probable that they would remain in that condition for another century. But they have not.

Communication with the outside world has opened up. Railways have been built for coal. Water power has been developed for factories. The isolation is broken. These surviving pioneers have been startled out of their wilderness privacy. The currents of the world's activities are already surging in upon them. They must learn quickly to navigate in these contending currents, or they will be swept away,—all but the few strong swimmers that would survive in any waters.

Their fathers and grandfathers have lived in their seclusion a life of idyllic leisure. If they had no books, few schools, and fewer comforts or conveniences, they did not greatly miss them. They were equal to all the demands that the simple wilderness life made upon them. But their successors today, with only their fathers' meager equipment, are not at all equal to the demands of the complex civilization now rushing upon them.

They have already suffered sorely in the ways of the world from the severe pressure of a gigantic and complicated social machinery at which they gazed in childlike wonder. They were not even afraid. They did not know it would devour them. So they were deprived of their timber, coal, and oil lands. Legally, of course, quite legally! It was as easy as stealing candy from a baby.

Unless their conscientious fellow citizens can

recognize the sudden tide that has swept in upon them, they will be overwhelmed. All the forces of uplift, of enlightenment, of succor, must give instant and energetic help, or they will become hewers of wood and drawers of water. They cannot with their bare hands cope with a civilization armed to the teeth with machinery. How can Daniel Boone, notwithstanding his personal charm and gentle wisdom, compete with the scientific inventiveness of Edison, or the organizing shrewdness of Rockefeller? Unsympathizing lawyers snatched Boone's lands from him again and again and finally drove him across the Mississippi into Spanish territory. Is a similar disgrace to be perpetrated upon his descendants today? They must be counselled and assisted by wise and disinterested leadership. They must be hastily prepared to meet the emergency that has burst in upon them and taken them by surprise. The educational process must be speeded up.

Perhaps the greatest possible help is friendly counsel. This cannot be issued to them in a government bulletin. It must come through personal and prolonged contact with those in whom they have learned to have confidence. They have, unfortunately, learned that most outsiders penetrating into the Mountains are looking out for their own selfish interests.

During recent years there has been a notable change, or at least the beginning of a change in meeting this inarticulate need. The most alert and forward-looking workers of various church boards, together with some independent workers, have started various kinds of *community work*. All of these centers and the people that man them are presumably working on the same general plan. Their fundamental purpose is not to do things for the community, much less to compete with other helpful agencies. Their aim is rather to link up the community with all the existing agencies; to give expert counsel so that the community shall not let its opportunities slip; to help it catch step with the available movements for betterment: the state board of education, its promoters and supervisors; the state university and its extension workers; the agricultural experiment station and its traveling advisers; the state board of health and its campaign of cooperation; national organizations offering help in district nursing, health teaching, clinics for hookworm, trachoma, tuberculosis, care of teeth, care of babies; thrift campaigns, credit unions, and many others.[1]

We make here brief mention of a few instances of community work that might well be taken as

[1] American Child Health Association, American Red Cross, Credit Union National Extension Bureau, Daughters of the American Revolution, National Education Association, National Organization for Public Health Nursing, Pi Beta Phi Fraternity, Rockefeller Sanitary Commission, Russell Sage Foundation, Southern Industrial Educational Association, State Federation of Women's Clubs, U. S. Departments of Agriculture, Education, Health, Children's Bureau, Young Men's Christian Association, Young Women's Christian Association.

patterns by all those trying to help the Mountain People solve their problem. The kind of work that should be undertaken depends partly upon the community under consideration, partly upon the finances available, and largely upon the personality and resourcefulness of the worker that undertakes it.

Here is a comfortable log cabin built midway between two district schoolhouses, one a mile and a half up the creek, the other as far below. Besides the two women that teach these schools—and that are paid by the public school fund—there is a housekeeper who also lives in the cabin. In addition to caring for the teachers she is a friendly visitor and counsellor in all the homes. She conducts a class for girls in sewing and, during the summer, in canning. As she becomes acquainted, she gives informal instruction to mothers in the care of children, sanitation, home nursing, and diet for the sick. Her support, of course, comes from outside sources.

Here is a similar log cabin with an extra room or two. This is the headquarters of a nurse, and the extra rooms are her tiny hospital. They are supplied with whatever conveniences the situation permits. Serious cases that need skilful nursing are brought here. The nurse visits the homes in the whole neighborhood, helping in sickness, dressing wounds, suggesting diet, and encouraging better sanitation. She cooperates loyally with the local physician (if the term *local* can be applied to a doctor living fifteen miles away). In some cases there is a medical woman, a licensed physician, as well as a nurse, living in the hospital. The teachers of the adjacent district schools may live there also. Various combinations are obviously possible. A leader of recreation sometimes resides in one of these settlements. Such a worker is of especial value where many families have gathered about a mine or a factory.

Very valuable assistance is given by volunteer workers in supervising a number of district schools in one corner of the county. A wise expert, by studying the different problems of each district teacher and by sympathetic understanding of each teacher's personality, can help a group of teachers to accomplish wonders in their own work with the pupils and in their influence over the communities in getting everybody to work together for a better school. After such volunteer supervisors have for a year or two given this valuable help to the public schools, the county in most cases will be glad to assume the burden of its support.

The work that most of the church boards have undertaken in the Mountains has naturally been schools and in many cases a school was the only open door to a community. In any case, it has carried the most immediate appeal; for who could resist helping the children? It gave also the quickest results, for children can be molded more readily than adults.

Here is an orphanage, undertaken in the belief that most rapid progress can be made when children are taken completely out of their original surroundings and transplanted into a completely new environment.

Other workers with similar convictions establish boarding schools, so that they may be able to influence the children twenty-four hours a day. They accept no pupils that live at home and require all to remain on the school grounds except for occasional visits home over stated Sundays.

It is a temptation to all educators to draw apart from the community and build an invisible cloister wall around himself and his pupils. He has constantly to correct the bread-and-butter emphasis which slights the invisible and intellectual in favor of material values. In counteracting and correcting this, he sometimes minimizes the legitimate value of practical affairs. In protecting his school from the control of mere earning capacity, he frequently releases the community from its responsibility for the moral and financial support of the school that they ought to carry.

In the beginning, with no adequate school on the horizon, it was doubtless necessary to establish some schools without waiting for the cooperation of the community. But as soon as the people got a taste of education, more and more responsibility should have been placed upon them. If a community is not enlisted in the work of the school, it will come to look upon it as a "pork barrel," a source of revenue to be shrewdly tapped whenever occasion offers. A school that has not won the moral and financial support of the community is a failure, even though many individual pupils have received great benefit. If the community cannot supply all the money to carry on a school, it should supply *all it can*. By its maximum contribution of money, and perhaps still more by regular consultation and advice about the actual administration of the school, the community must take its share of the responsibility and give its moral and spiritual support to the whole work of the school.

The most pressing educational need is for elementary instruction that is practical enough and ideal enough for mature minds. The schools operating under the Smith-Hughes bill are a step suggesting the right direction.

Studies must be chosen that are seen to have a direct connection with life *as viewed by the pupil*. And they must be taught in such a way that, with every effort he makes, the student achieves a recognizable progress in the art of living.

The constant aim of the instructor should be to help the pupil acquire the power to make things. To attain creative power is the end of all education, whether it be ability to make a rabbit trap or to compose an oratorio. For this reason there should be intelligent and enthusiastic guidance in hand work *in the elementary grades*. The average age of pupils in the Mountain schools is much older than elsewhere. Boys and girls of fifteen are common in the fourth grade. For this reason, schools should be equipped to teach boys and girls the use of all sorts of tools and the management and control of all sorts of processes. These should include sewing and woodworking, drawing and basketry, cooking and weaving, the rudiments of gardening, farming, and domestic architecture.

Between twenty and thirty million dollars a year is given for higher education in the United States. Is there no far-seeing philanthropist who will give a few millions for carefully directed elementary or secondary education? There is no finer field for experimentation than the virgin spaces of Appalachia.

How fascinating to build such a school far back in the mountains, perhaps ten miles from even a lumber railway. The buildings, whether of stone, or logs, or sawed lumber, should be rustic rather than citified. They should have all suitable conveniences, of course. Most of all they should be beautiful; everything about them should be in harmony with the wilderness setting.

A stone dam three hundred feet up the mountain side would gather water for the kitchen, dormitories, and barn. A turbine in the main pipe would furnish electric light. The overflow would provide a swimming pool.

There should be a practical agricultural department, with a model garden in the richest level spot. This would furnish all the vegetables the kitchen could use, fresh and canned, and would also afford some little plots for the individual experiments of various classes learning to grow vegetables. The site chosen should include a good meadow level enough for a mowing machine, rich bottom land for corn, gentle slopes for pasture, and an acre or so for fruit trees and grape vines. A coal mine in the mountain and plenty of timber on it should not be overlooked. A model barn would house the animals and their feed. It is important that there should be a construction department whose director would teach the boys (and neighbors) simple carpentry, blacksmith work, stone cutting and masonry, pipe fitting and painting. There should, of course, be a department of household arts to teach the girls cooking, weaving, nursing, gardening, and the making of furniture. Equally important would be supervised recreation, outdoor games, the playing of some musical instrument, drawing, singing, dancing, dramatization, woodcraft, including a knowledge of flowers, trees, and birds.

At one edge of the school grounds would stand a little hospital with a dozen beds and—a nurse.

She would give instruction in cleanliness, sanitation, diet, health habits, first aid, and home nursing. In the community she would conduct individual clinics in the care of babies, and give instruction in the nourishing of children, school lunches, and diet for convalescents. Possibly, by furnishing suitable quarters, a physician might be secured to reside there.

Cottages should be built instead of large dormitories. Attempts made anywhere to educate on a wholesale scale are too often malpractice; it is always so in the Mountains.

Much use should be made of a library. Books, magazines, framed pictures, farmers' bulletins, should be circulated in the community as well as among the pupils. A debating club should be encouraged for young men not in school, and a farmers' meeting held, perhaps, on Saturday evenings. A recognized part of the program should be "continuation classes" to give the people of the community what they want—whether it be plumbing or poetry, road-building or Rembrandt.

The school curriculum should cover not more than four years—let us say from the ninth through the twelfth grade. At first there would doubtless need to be a coach class for those weak in the eighth grade, but it is usually unwise to include too great diversity of work or of pupils in one school. Four years is a broad enough unit. What shall the boys and girls study? Language, literature, history, mathematics (including simplified surveying, levelling, mechanics, and the elements of road engineering), the foundations of science, and in the last year some sociology and pedagogy. The aim of the school being to build citizenship, it should develop men and women with the habit of thinking, with skill to do, and with the ability to live together in free and helpful community life.

It would be difficult to find teachers and workers with enough breadth, energy, and initiative to carry on work so different from the conventional schools in which most of us grew up. The worker must be practical and resourceful, or he could not successfully meet the severe conditions of the isolated life. He must be able to stand alone, and yet work readily with others. He must be keen, yet kindly, with fraternal tact and abundant common sense. He should be spiritual rather than pious, sensitive to the presence of God rather than valiant in defending the faith. A man that appreciates beauty in the rough and sees possibilities that are not yet visible! No man of mediocre ability, conventional in mind and morals, should be sent to the Mountains, no matter how willing or zealous he be for service. Send only those that can discriminate between what is essential and what is incidental in our modern civilization; men with insight to interpret the great movements of the past and to discern in the present cross-currents the direction of the great movements of the future.

They must be men and women that know the Mountain People, their history, their environment, their aspirations; men and women so well acquainted with Mountain life that they do not mistake for essential features the accidental peculiarities or oddities that catch the attention of the casual visitor. They must be people with understanding sympathy, with a genuine sense of kinship, with fellow-feeling—not sentimentality.

Men too crude for the city will fail here. The situation demands men and women of culture, who enjoy the world's best; men and women with deep appreciation of beauty in painting, music, architecture, and poetry; men and women with vivid social sense, and a vital interest in the upheavings of democracy, with a moral passion for righteousness coupled with invincible patience and unbreakable hopefulness. Only such can help the Mountain People to enter into their belated heritage.

Scattered here and there are notable examples of cooperation in some community betterment. Usually such cooperation is the outgrowth of the community's confidence in one person; confidence in his (or frequently her) integrity, in his practical judgment, in his understanding sympathy, to which they bear glad witness, by saying "he's a mighty common man."

There are many cases of a school being so fortunate as to have secured a succession of wise, friendly, devoted workers. Such an institution wins the confidence of a wide scope of territory. Its reputation and influence extend far beyond the range of personal acquaintance. If it can constantly obtain a succession of new workers of persistent friendliness and intelligent neighborliness, its beneficent influence will continue widespread. To secure and develop such workers is difficult, and most schools fall away from their primitive neighborliness and become institutionalized and dehumanized. But so far and so long as the worker's interest is genuine, unselfish, and deep, the community will trust him and follow his leading if he have the ability to lead.

One of the most hopeful projects for community betterment has recently been launched by one of the larger schools. To give an initial impetus it secured from a friend two prizes, one of three thousand, and one of two thousand dollars, to be awarded to the counties making most progress in eighteen months. It issued a pamphlet of instructions and the system of grading for the contest, and sent its workers to assist in organizing the competing counties. Expecting to enroll three or four, it has finally admitted ten counties.

A county competing may improve along ten lines, gaining the following points: schools, two thousand points; health and sanitation, one thousand; home and farm, one thousand; church and Sunday school, one thousand; agriculture and livestock, one thousand; community clubs, five hundred; boys' and girls' clubs, one thousand; roads and public buildings, one thousand; newspapers and magazines, five hundred; and social work, one thousand.

Hearty cooperation is given by the State Department of Education, the State Board of Health, the State Agricultural College, the National Red Cross, and other organizations.

No county can enter the contest until an agreement to push improvement is signed by the County Judge and the Fiscal Court, the County Health officer, the Board of Education, the county farm agent and a committee of representative ministers. The school's Extension Committee acts as a clearing house to get the local officials in touch with the state or national forces that make for progress.

Each county is surveyed and its standing in the ten departments evaluated at the beginning of the contest. From this, its progress during the eighteen months' duration of the contest is measured. For instance, under "Schools" three hundred points can be made by improved attendance, points for employing teachers with high school, normal school, or college training, points for increasing teachers' salaries, points for new school buildings or equipment.

Under Health and Sanitation a "standard store" is defined as a store having fly screens on doors and windows, food protected against dust and flies, no spittoons, and no spitting on floor, facilities for clerks to wash their hands frequently, and floors oiled at least four times a year. Standards set for post offices, court houses, railroad stations and other public buildings will educate the public. People that are hopelessly indifferent to these ideals will do considerable to beat an adjoining county. Under school sanitation, points are given for medical inspection of individual schools and for supervised play.

Improvements in homes include the painting of houses or barns, installing kitchen sinks, water in the house, refrigerators, separators, washing machines, sewing machines, sewing and weaving, sheds for machinery, cellars, and new fences. A "standard home" must have safe drainage, not less than three rooms for two people, one room more for each additional two, doors and windows screened, water (pronounced safe by State Board of Health) within ten yards of the kitchen door, a sanitary outhouse, and a yard free from rubbish and weeds. Points are assigned for better stock, sheep, hogs, cattle, and poultry, for vaccination and inoculation, for planting fruit trees, and improving gardens, for putting in tile drains, sowing legumes, testing seed, or producing eggs in quantity.

In most cases the chairmen of these ten departments are the officials naturally in charge: the county superintendent of schools, the county health officer of sanitation, the county agent of farm improvement and boys' clubs, the county home demonstration agent of homes and girls' clubs, the fiscal court of roads, and an elected committee representing the churches. Under the stimulus of the contest these officials learn better how to do their work, the people eagerly support them, and efficiency almost becomes a habit. County nurses, farm agents, home demonstration agents, are appointed. Bond issues are voted to build roads, Sunday schools are organized, and new churches are built.

Contesting counties that do not win the money prize will win a greater prize in the experience of working together to reach a higher standard in many departments that make rural life better.

There is great opportunity in the Mountains for helpers that have the Pauline ability to earn their own living more or less incidentally. A doctor that is not afraid of pioneer conditions can go into the Land of Saddle-bags and earn his living. Any sort of general tradesman, *if he have initiative*, can earn his own expenses without the support of a church board, and by brotherly living he can leaven the neighborhood for cooperative and community betterment.

There is one consideration that has been largely

The Challenge 259

overlooked by those literary folk that have written about the Mountain People. I refer to the emigration from the Mountains. This was of two kinds. In the earlier days, as has been noted in Chapter Three, there was a definite movement of population, an observable stream of migration. This flowed from western Pennsylvania down the valley of Virginia to Carolina. There it turned westward through Tennessee and at Cumberland Gap poured into Kentucky. This stream flowed along certain channels, and, as is the way with full, strong-moving, swollen streams, there was considerable splashing over the edges, and sometimes distinct little rivulets trickled through the banks. Thus many families were separated from the main stream and settled on either side all along its way. The farther the migration flowed, the more strongly its waters washed over the banks, so that in the southwest, the population at the foot of the mountains was very largely impregnated by the stream of commingled Scotch-Irish, Virginia English, Palatine German and French Huguenot, the main stream of which became the Appalachian population that we call the Mountain People. Thus James Robertson flowed off to Nashville, Abraham Lincoln's father was washed into the foothills of Kentucky (Abraham was born in Hardin County) and drifted thence to Indiana and Illinois. Daniel Boone and several of his sons were borne on a stronger current into the Spanish possessions of Missouri. Davy Crockett and Sam Houston were swept as far as Texas.

Such currents of migration represented by the well-known men mentioned spread over the mountains and overflowed the adjacent areas, leaving a rich deposit of valiant pioneer manhood.

The straight-grained, hardy, wholesome-minded mountain stock has, therefore, already contributed largely to the nation of its sterling Anglo-Saxon and Anglo-Celtic qualities.

The second kind of emigration referred to is individual. True to the original exploring type, strong-minded and venturesome men have continually left the Mountains and gone out to try their fortunes in other places. Numberless young Lincolns have built their lives into towns and villages all over the nation and have enriched the community life with their homespun virtues and rugged strength.

Out of this mountain reservoir can be drawn a constant stream of vigorous native manhood and charmingly simple womanhood, fresh, unjaded, unspoiled, and in the deepest sense, American. American in language, ideals and religion. American in their love of freedom. American in their fearlessness of the future. American in their resourcefulness and adaptability. American most of all, perhaps, in their unspoiled neighborliness and hospitality.

www.ingramcontent.com/pod-product-compliance
Lightning Source LLC
Chambersburg PA
CBHW020331240426
43665CB00043B/216